The Plays of W. E. Henley and R. L. Stevenson

William Ernest Henley is most noted for his poetry of which he wrote several volumes with the outstanding contribution being the poem 'Invictus'

His life was overshadowed by a great deal of ill health and although he died at the young age of 53 he contributed much to Victorian literature.

His partner in the plays we publish here made a somewhat greater contribution to the literary world. Indeed in the Scottish canon to be placed alongside Burns is high praise indeed but it's a rightful place for one of Scotland's finest novelists. Born in 1850 he managed to cram much into his 44 years travelling widely to France, the United States, Samoa and the South Seas. Of course he is widely feted for his classics Dr Jeckyll & Mr Hyde, Treasure Island and poetry volumes such as A Child's Garden Of Verses.

Together these two fine minds bring us some largely forgotten works which we are pleased to publish here.

Index Of Contents
PAGE DEACON BRODIE
BEAU AUSTIN
ADMIRAL GUINEA
ROBERT MACAIRE

DEACON BRODIE OR THE DOUBLE LIFE A MELODRAMA IN FIVE ACTS AND EIGHT TABLEAUX

PERSONS REPRESENTED
WILLIAM BRODIE, Deacon of the Wrights, Housebreaker and Master Carpenter.
OLD BRODIE, the Deacon's Father.
WILLIAM LAWSON, Procurator-Fiscal, the Deacon's Uncle.
ANDREW AINSLIE, HUMPHREY MOORE, GEORGE SMITH, Robbers in the Deacon's gang.
CAPTAIN RIVERS, an English Highwayman.
HUNT, a Bow Street Runner.
A DOCTOR.
WALTER LESLIE.
MARY BRODIE, the Deacon's Sister.
JEAN WATT, the Deacon's Mistress.
VAGABONDS, OFFICERS OF THE WATCH, MEN-SERVANTS.

The Scene is laid in Edinburgh. The Time is towards the close of the Eighteenth Century. The Action, some fifty hours long, begins at eight p.m. on Saturday and ends before midnight on Monday.

NOTE.—Passages suggested for omission in representation are enclosed in square brackets, thus [ ].

SYNOPSIS OF ACTS AND TABLEAUX
ACT I.
TABLEAU I.   The Double Life.
TABLEAU II.   Hunt the Runner.
TABLEAU III.   Mother Clarke's.
ACT II.
TABLEAU IV.   Evil and Good.
ACT III.
TABLEAU V.   King's Evidence.
TABLEAU VI.   Unmasked.
ACT IV.
TABLEAU VII.   The Robbery.
ACT V.
TABLEAU VIII. The Open Door.

LONDON: PRINCE'S THEATRE

2d July 1884

DEACON BRODIE,   Mr. E. J. HENLEY.
WALTER LESLIE,   Mr. CHARLES CARTWRIGHT.
WILLIAM LAWSON,   Mr. JOHN MACLEAN.
ANDREW AINSLIE,   Mr. FRED DESMOND.
HUMPHREY MOORE,   Mr. EDMUND GRACE.
GEORGE SMITH,   Mr. JULIAN CROSS.
HUNT,   Mr. HUBERT AKHURST.
OLD BRODIE,   Mr. A. KNIGHT.
CAPTAIN RIVERS,   Mr. BRANDON THOMAS.
MARY BRODIE,   Miss LIZZIE WILLIAMS.
JEAN WATT,   Miss MINNIE BELL.

MONTREAL

26th September 1887

DEACON BRODIE,   Mr. E. J. HENLEY.
WALTER LESLIE,   Mr. GRAHAM STEWART.
WILLIAM LAWSON,   Mr. EDMUND LYONS.
ANDREW AINSLIE,   Mr. FRED DESMOND.
HUMPHREY MOORE,   Mr. EDMUND GRACE.
GEORGE SMITH,   Mr. HORATIO SAKER.
HUNT,   Mr. HENRY VERNON.
CAPTAIN RIVERS,   Mr. BRUCE PHILIPS.
MARY BRODIE,   Miss ANNIE ROBE.
JEAN WATT,   Miss CARRIE COOTE.

ACT I.

TABLEAU I. THE DOUBLE LIFE.

The Stage represents a room in the Deacon's house, furnished partly as a sitting-, partly as a bed-room, in the style of an easy burgess of about 1780. C., a door; L. C., a second and smaller door; R. C., practicable window; L., alcove, supposed to contain bed; at the back, a clothes-press and a corner cupboard containing bottles, etc. MARY BRODIE at needlework; OLD BRODIE, a paralytic, in wheeled chair, at the fireside, L.

SCENE I

To these LESLIE, C.

LESLIE. May I come in, Mary?

MARY. Why not?

LESLIE. I scarce knew where to find you.

MARY. The dad and I must have a corner, must we not? So when my brother's friends are in the parlour he allows us to sit in his room. 'Tis a great favour, I can tell you; the place is sacred.

LESLIE. Are you sure that 'sacred' is strong enough?

MARY. You are satirical!

LESLIE. I? And with regard to the Deacon? Believe me, I am not so ill-advised. You have trained me well, and I feel by him as solemnly as a true-born Brodie.

MARY. And now you are impertinent! Do you mean to go any further? We are a fighting race, we Brodies. Oh, you may laugh, sir! But 'tis no child's play to jest us on our Deacon, or, for that matter, on our Deacon's chamber either. It was his father's before him: he works in it by day and sleeps in it by night; and scarce anything it contains but is the labour of his hands. Do you see this table, Walter? He made it while he was yet a 'prentice. I remember how I used to sit and watch him at his work. It would be grand, I thought, to be able to do as he did, and handle edge-tools without cutting my fingers, and getting my ears pulled for a meddlesome minx! He used to give me his mallet to keep and his nails to hold; and didn't I fly when he called for them! and wasn't I proud to be ordered about with them! And then, you know, there is the tall cabinet yonder; that it was that proved him the first of Edinburgh joiners, and worthy to be their Deacon and their head. And the father's chair, and the sister's workbox, and the dear dead mother's footstool—what are they all but proofs of the Deacon's skill, and tokens of the Deacon's care for those about him?

LESLIE. I am all penitence. Forgive me this last time, and I promise you I never will again.

MARY. Candidly, now, do you think you deserve forgiveness?

LESLIE. Candidly, I do not.

MARY. Then I suppose you must have it. What have you done with Willie and my uncle?

LESLIE. I left them talking deeply. The dear old Procurator has not much thought just now for anything but those mysterious burglaries—

MARY. I know!—

LESLIE. Still, all of him that is not magistrate and official is politician and citizen; and he has been striving his hardest to undermine the Deacon's principles, and win the Deacon's vote and interest.

MARY. They are worth having, are they not?

LESLIE. The Procurator seems to think that having them makes the difference between winning and losing.

MARY. Did he say so? You may rely upon it that he knows. There are not many in Edinburgh who can match with our Will.

LESLIE. There shall be as many as you please, and not one more.

MARY. How I should like to have heard you! What did uncle say? Did he speak of the Town Council again? Did he tell Will what a wonderful Bailie he would make? O why did you come away?

LESLIE. I could not pretend to listen any longer. The election is months off yet; and if it were not—if it were tramping upstairs this moment—drums, flags, cockades, guineas, candidates, and all!—how should I care for it? What are Whig and Tory to me?

MARY. O fie on you! It is for every man to concern himself in the common weal. Mr. Leslie—Leslie of the Craig!—should know that much at least.

LESLIE. And be a politician like the Deacon? All in good time, but not now. I hearkened while I could, and when I could no more I slipped out and followed my heart. I hoped I should be welcome.

MARY. I suppose you mean to be unkind.

LESLIE. Tit for tat. Did you not ask me why I came away? And is it usual for a young lady to say 'Mr.' to the man she means to marry?

MARY. That is for the young lady to decide, sir.

LESLIE. And against that judgment there shall be no appeal?

MARY. O, if you mean to argue!

LESLIE. I do not mean to argue. I am content to love and be loved. I think I am the happiest man in the world.

MARY. That is as it should be; for I am the happiest girl.

LESLIE. Why not say the happiest wife? I have your word, and you have mine. Is not that enough?

MARY. Have you so soon forgotten? Did I not tell you how it must be as my brother wills? I can do only as he bids me.

LESLIE. Then you have not spoken as you promised?

MARY. I have been too happy to speak.

LESLIE. I am his friend. Precious as you are, he will trust you to me. He has but to know how I love you, Mary, and how your life is all in your love of me, to give us his blessing with a full heart.

MARY. I am sure of him. It is that which makes my happiness complete. Even to our marriage I should find it hard to say 'Yes' when he said 'No.'

LESLIE. Your father is trying to speak. I'll wager he echoes you.

MARY (to OLD BRODIE). My poor dearie! Do you want to say anything to me? No? Is it to Mr. Leslie, then?

LESLIE. I am listening, Mr. Brodie.

MARY. What is it, daddie?

OLD BRODIE. My son—the Deacon—Deacon Brodie—the first at school.

LESLIE. I know it, Mr. Brodie. Was I not the last in the same class? (To MARY.) But he seems to have forgotten us.

MARY. O yes! his mind is wellnigh gone. He will sit for hours as you see him, and never speak nor stir but at the touch of Will's hand or the sound of Will's name.

LESLIE. It is so good to sit beside you. By and by it will be always like this. You will not let me speak to the Deacon? You are fast set upon speaking yourself? I could be so eloquent, Mary—I would touch him. I cannot tell you how I fear to trust my happiness to any one else—even to you!

MARY. He must hear of my good fortune from none but me. And besides, you do not understand. We are not like families, we Brodies. We are so clannish, we hold so close together.

LESLIE. You Brodies, and your Deacon!

OLD BRODIE. Deacon of his craft, sir—Deacon of the Wrights—my son! If his mother—his mother—had but lived to see!

MARY. You hear how he runs on. A word about my brother and he catches it. 'Tis as if he were awake in his poor blind way to all the Deacon's care for him and all the Deacon's kindness to me. I believe he only lives in the thought of the Deacon. There, it is not so long since I was one with him. But indeed I think we are all Deacon-mad, we Brodies. Are we not, daddie dear?

BRODIE (without, and entering). You are a mighty magistrate, Procurator, but you seem to have met your match.

SCENE II

To these, BRODIE and LAWSON.

MARY (curtseying). So, uncle! you have honoured us at last.

LAWSON. Quam primum, my dear, quam primum.

BRODIE. Well, father, do you know me? (He sits beside his father and takes his hand.)

[OLD BRODIE. William—ay—Deacon. Greater man—than—his father.

BRODIE. You see, Procurator, the news is as fresh to him as it was five years ago. He was struck down before he got the Deaconship, and lives his lost life in mine.

LAWSON. Ay, I mind. He was aye ettling after a bit handle to his name. He was kind of hurt when first they made me Procurator.]

MARY. And what have you been talking of?

LAWSON. Just o' thae robberies, Mary. Baith as a burgher and a Crown offeecial, I tak' the maist absorbing interest in thae robberies.

LESLIE. Egad, Procurator, and so do I.

BRODIE (with a quick look at LESLIE). A dilettante interest, doubtless! See what it is to be idle.

LESLIE. Faith, Brodie, I hardly know how to style it.

BRODIE. At any rate, 'tis not the interest of a victim, or we should certainly have known of it before; nor a practical tool-mongering interest, like my own; nor an interest professional and official, like the Procurator's. You can answer for that, I suppose?

LESLIE. I think I can; if for no more. It's an interest of my own, you see, and is best described as indescribable, and of no manner of moment to anybody. [It will take no hurt if we put off its discussion till a month of Sundays.]

BRODIE. You are more fortunate than you deserve. What do you say, Procurator?

LAWSON. Ay is he! There is no a house in Edinburgh safe. The law is clean helpless, clean helpless! A week syne it was auld Andra Simpson's in the Lawnmarket. Then, naething would set the catamarans but to forgather privily wi' the Provost's ain butler, and tak' unto themselves the Provost's ain plate. And the day, information was laid before me offeecially that the limmers had made infraction, vi et clam, into Leddy Mar'get Dalziel's, and left her leddyship wi' no sae muckle's a spune to sup her parritch wi'. It's unbelievable, it's awful, it's anti-christian!

MARY. If you only knew them, uncle, what an example you would make! But tell me, is it not strange that men should dare such things, in the midst of a city, and nothing, nothing be known of them—nothing at all?

LESLIE. Little, indeed! But we do know that there are several in the gang, and that one at least is an unrivalled workman.

LAWSON. Yo're right, sir; ye're vera right, Mr. Leslie. It had been deponed to me offeecially that no a tradesman—no the Deacon here himsel'—could have made a cleaner job wi' Andra Simpson's shutters. And as for the lock o' the bank—but that's an auld sang.

BRODIE. I think you believe too much, Procurator. Rumour's an ignorant jade, I tell you. I've had occasion to see some little of their handiwork—broken cabinets, broken shutters, broken doors—and I find them bunglers. Why, I could do it better myself!

LESLIE. Gad, Brodie, you and I might go into partnership. I back myself to watch outside, and I suppose you could do the work of skill within?

BRODIE. An opposition company? Leslie, your mind is full of good things. Suppose we begin to-night, and give the Procurator's house the honours of our innocence?

MARY. You could do anything, you two!

LAWSON. Onyway, Deacon, ye'd put your ill-gotten gains to a right use; they might come by the wind but they wouldna gang wi' the water; and that's aye a solatium, as we say. If I am to be robbit, I would like to be robbit wi' decent folk; and no think o' my bonnie clean siller dirling among jads and dicers. [Faith, William, the mair I think on't, the mair I'm o' Mr. Leslie's mind. Come the night, or come the morn, and I'se gie ye my free permission, and lend ye a hand in at the window forbye!

BRODIE. Come, come, Procurator, lead not our poor clay into temptation. (LESLIE and MARY talk apart.)

LAWSON. I'm no muckle afraid for your puir clay, as ye ca't.] But hark i' your ear: ye're likely, joking apart, to be gey and sune in partnership wi' Mr. Leslie. He and Mary are gey and pack, a body can see that.

[BRODIE. 'Daffin' and want o' wit'—you know the rest.

LAWSON. Vidi, scivi, et audivi, as we say in a Sasine, William.] Man, because my wig's pouthered do ye think I havena a green heart? I was aince a lad mysel', and I ken fine by the glint o' the e'e when a lad's fain and a lassie's willing. And, man, it's the town's talk; communis error fit jus, ye ken.

[OLD BRODIE. Oh!

LAWSON. See, ye're hurting your faither's hand.

BRODIE. Dear dad, it is not good to have an ill-tempered son.

LAWSON. What the deevil ails ye at the match? 'Od, man, he has a nice bit divot o' Fife corn-land, I can tell ye, and some Bordeaux wine in his cellar! But I needna speak o' the Bordeaux; ye'll ken the smack o't as weel's I do mysel'; onyway it's grand wine. Tantum et tale. I tell ye the pro's, find you the con.'s, if ye're able.]

BRODIE. [I am sorry, Procurator, but I must be short with you.] You are talking in the air, as lawyers will. I prefer to drop the subject [and it will displease me if you return to it in my hearing].

LESLIE. At four o'clock to-morrow? At my house? (to MARY).

MARY. As soon as church is done. (EXIT MARY.)

LAWSON. Ye needna be sae high and mighty, onyway.

BRODIE. I ask your pardon, Procurator. But we Brodies—you know our failings! [A bad temper and a humour of privacy.]

LAWSON. Weel, I maun be about my business. But I could tak' a doch-an-dorach, William; superflua non nocent, as we say; an extra dram hurts naebody, Mr. Leslie.

BRODIE (with bottle and glasses). Here's your old friend, Procurator. Help yourself, Leslie. Oh no, thank you, not any for me. You strong people have the advantage of me there. With my attacks, you know, I must always live a bit of a hermit's life.

LAWSON. 'Od, man, that's fine; that's health o' mind and body. Mr. Leslie, here's to you, sir. 'Od, it's harder to end than to begin wi' stuff like that.

SCENE III

To these, SMITH and JEAN, C.

SMITH. Is the king of the castle in, please?

LAWSON (aside). Lord's sake, it's Smith!

BRODIE (to SMITH). I beg your pardon?

SMITH. I beg yours, sir. If you please, sir, is Mr. Brodie at home, sir?

BRODIE. What do you want with him, my man?

SMITH. I've a message for him, sir, a job of work, sir!

BRODIE (to SMITH; referring to JEAN). And who is this?

JEAN. I am here for the Procurator, about my rent. There's nae offence, I hope, sir.

LAWSON. It's just an honest wife I let a flat to in Libberton's Wynd. It'll be for the rent?

JEAN. Just that, sir.

LAWSON. Weel, ye can just bide here a wee, and I'll step down the road to my office wi' ye. (Exeunt BRODIE, LAWSON, LESLIE, C.)

SCENE IV

SMITH, JEAN WATT, OLD BRODIE.

SMITH (bowing them out). Your humble and most devoted servant, George Smith, Esquire. And so this is the garding, is it? And this is the style of horticulture? Ha, it is! (At the mirror.) In that case George's mother bids him bind his hair. (Kisses his hand.) My dearest Duchess,—(To JEAN.) I say, Jean, there's a good deal of difference between this sort of thing and the way we does it in Libberton's Wynd.

JEAN. I daursay. And what wad ye expeck?

SMITH. Ah, Jean, if you'd cast affection's glance on this poor but honest soger! George Lord S. is not the nobleman to cut the object of his flame before the giddy throng; nor to keep her boxed up in an old mouse-trap, while he himself is revelling in purple splendours like these. He didn't know you, Jean: he was afraid to. Do you call that a man? Try a man that is.

JEAN. Geordie Smith, ye ken vera weel I'll tak' nane o' that sort of talk frae you. And what kind o' a man are you to even yoursel' to the likes o' him? He's a gentleman.

SMITH. Ah, ain't he just! And don't he live up to it? I say, Jean, feel of this chair.

JEAN. My! look at yon bed!

SMITH. The carpet too! Axminster, by the bones of Oliver Cromwell!

JEAN. What a expense!

SMITH. Hey, brandy! The deuce of the grape! Have a toothful, Mrs. Watt. [(Sings)—

'Says Bacchus to Venus,
There's brandy between us,
And the cradle of love is the bowl, the bowl!']

JEAN. Nane for me, I thank ye, Mr. Smith.

SMITH. What brings the man from stuff like this to rotgut and spittoons at Mother Clarke's; but ah, George, you was born for a higher spear! And so was you, Mrs. Watt, though I say it that shouldn't. (Seeing OLD BRODIE for the first time.) Hullo! it's a man!

JEAN. Thonder in the chair. (They go to look at him, their backs to the door.)

GEORGE. Is he alive?

JEAN. I think there's something wrong with him.

GEORGE. And how was you to-morrow, my valued old gentleman, eh?

JEAN. Dinna mak' a mock o' him, Geordie.

OLD BRODIE. My son—the Deacon—Deacon of his trade.

JEAN. He'll be his feyther. (HUNT appears at door C., and stands looking on.)

SMITH. The Deacon's old man! Well, he couldn't expect to have his quiver full of sich, could he, Jean? (To OLD BRODIE.) Ah, my Christian soldier, if you had, the world would have been more varigated. Mrs. Deakin (to JEAN), let me introduce you to your dear papa.

JEAN. Think shame to yoursel'! This is the Deacon's house; you and me shouldna be here by rights; and if we are, it's the least we can do to behave dacent. [This is no the way ye'll mak' me like ye.]

SMITH. All right, Duchess. Don't be angry.

SCENE V

To these, HUNT, C. (He steals down, and claps each one suddenly on the shoulder.)

HUNT. Is there a gentleman here by the name of Mr. Procurator-Fiscal?

SMITH (pulling himself together). D—n it, Jerry, what do you mean by startling an old customer like that?

HUNT. What, my brave un'? You're the very party I was looking for!

SMITH. There's nothing out against me this time?

HUNT. I'll take odds there is. But it ain't in my hands. (To OLD BRODIE.) You'll excuse me, old genelman?

SMITH. Ah, well, if it's all in the way of friendship! . . . I say, Jean, [you and me had best be on the toddle.] We shall be late for church.

HUNT. Lady, George?

SMITH. It's a—yes, it's a lady. Come along, Jean.

HUNT. A Mrs. Deacon, I believe? [That was the name, I think?] Won't Mrs. Deacon let me have a queer at her phiz?

JEAN (unmuffling). I've naething to be ashamed of. My name's Mistress Watt; I'm weel kennt at the Wynd heid; there's naething again me.

HUNT. No, to be sure, there ain't; and why clap on the blinkers, my dear? You that has a face like a rose, and with a cove like Jerry Hunt that might be your born father? [But all this don't tell me about Mr. Procurator-Fiscal.]

GEORGE (in an agony). Jean, Jean, we shall be late. (Going with attempted swagger.) Well, ta-ta, Jerry.

SCENE VI

To these, C, BRODIE and LAWSON (greatcoat, muffler, lantern).

LAWSON (from the door). Come your ways, Mistress Watt.

JEAN. That's the Fiscal himsel'.

HUNT. Mr. Procurator-Fiscal, I believe?

LAWSON. That's me. Who'll you be?

HUNT. Hunt the Runner, sir; Hunt from Bow Street; English warrant.

LAWSON. There's a place for a' things, officer. Come your ways to my office, with me and this guid wife.

BRODIE (aside to JEAN, as she passes with a curtsey). How dare you be here? (Aloud to SMITH.) Wait you here, my man.

SMITH. If you please, sir. (BRODIE goes out, C.)

SCENE VII

BRODIE, SMITH.

BRODIE. What the devil brings you here?

SMITH. Confound it, Deakin! Not rusty?

[BRODIE. And not you only: Jean too! Are you mad?

SMITH. Why, you don't mean to say, Deakin, that you have been stodged by G. Smith, Esquire? Plummy old George?]

BRODIE. There was my uncle the Procurator—

SMITH. The Fiscal? He don't count.

BRODIE. What d'ye mean?

SMITH. Well, Deakin, since Fiscal Lawson's Nunkey Lawson, and it's all in the family way, I don't mind telling you that Nunkey Lawson's a customer of George's. We give Nunkey Lawson a good deal of brandy—G. S. and Co.'s celebrated Nantz.

BRODIE. What! does he buy that smuggled trash of yours?

SMITH. Well, we don't call it smuggled in the trade, Deakin. It's a wink, and King George's picter between G. S. and the Nunks.

BRODIE. Gad! that's worth knowing. O Procurator, Procurator, is there no such thing as virtue? [Allons! It's enough to cure a man of vice for this world and the other.] But hark you hither, Smith; this is all damned well in its way, but it don't explain what brings you here.

SMITH. I've trapped a pigeon for you.

BRODIE. Can't you pluck him yourself?

SMITH. Not me. He's too flash in the feather for a simple nobleman like George Lord Smith. It's the great Capting Starlight, fresh in from York. [He's exercised his noble art all the way from here to London. 'Stand and deliver, stap my vitals!'] And the north road is no bad lay, Deakin.

BRODIE. Flush?

SMITH (mimicking). 'The graziers, split me! A mail, stap my vitals! and seven demned farmers, by the Lard—'

BRODIE. By Gad!

SMITH. Good for trade, ain't it? And we thought, Deakin, the Badger and me, that coins being ever on the vanish, and you not over sweet on them there lovely little locks at Leslie's, and them there bigger and uglier marine stores at the Excise Office . . .

BRODIE (impossible). Go on.

SMITH. Worse luck! . . . We thought, me and the Badger, you know, that maybe you'd like to exercise your helbow with our free and galliant horseman.

BRODIE. The old move, I presume? the double set of dice?

SMITH. That's the rig, Deakin. What you drop on the square you pick up again on the cross. [Just as you did with G. S. and Co.'s own agent and correspondent, the Admiral from Nantz.] You always was a neat hand with the bones, Deakin.

BRODIE. The usual terms, I suppose?

SMITH. The old discount, Deakin. Ten in the pound for you, and the rest for your jolly companions every one. [That's the way we does it!]

BRODIE. Who has the dice?

SMITH. Our mutual friend, the Candleworm.

BRODIE. You mean Ainslie?—We trust that creature too much, Geordie.

SMITH. He's all right, Marquis. He wouldn't lay a finger on his own mother. Why, he's no more guile in him than a set of sheep's trotters.

[BRODIE. You think so? Then see he don't cheat you over the dice, and give you light for loaded. See to that, George, see to that; and you may count the Captain as bare as his last grazier.

SMITH. The Black Flag for ever! George'll trot him round to Mother Clarke's in two twos.] How long'll you be?

BRODIE. The time to lock up and go to bed, and I'll be with you. Can you find your way out?

SMITH. Bloom on, my Sweet William, in peaceful array. Ta-ta.

SCENE VIII

BRODIE, OLD BRODIE; to whom, MARY.

MARY. O Willie, I am glad you did not go with them. I have something to tell you. If you knew how happy I am, you would clap your hands, Will. But come, sit you down there, and be my good big brother, and I will kneel here and take your hand. We must keep close to dad, and then he will feel happiness in the air. The poor old love, if we could only tell him! But I sometimes think his heart has gone to heaven already, and takes a part in all our joys and sorrows; and it is only his poor body that remains here, helpless and ignorant. Come, Will, sit you down, and ask me questions—or guess—that will be better, guess.

BRODIE. Not to-night, Mary; not to-night. I have other fish to fry, and they won't wait.

MARY. Not one minute for your sister? One little minute for your little sister?

BRODIE. Minutes are precious, Mary. I have to work for all of us, and the clock is always busy. They are waiting for me even now. Help me with the dad's chair. And then to bed, and dream happy things. And to-morrow morning I will hear your news—your good news; it must be good, you look so proud and glad. But to-night it cannot be.

MARY. I hate your business—I hate all business. To think of chairs, and tables, and foot-rules, all dead and wooden—and cold pieces of money with the King's ugly head on them; and here is your sister, your pretty sister, if you please, with something to tell, which she would not tell you for the world, and would give the world to have you guess, and you won't?—Not you! For business! Fie, Deacon Brodie! But I'm too happy to find fault with you.

BRODIE. 'And me a Deacon,' as the Procurator would say.

MARY. No such thing, sir! I am not a bit afraid of you—nor a bit angry neither. Give me a kiss, and promise me hours and hours to-morrow morning.

BRODIE. All day long to-morrow, if you like.

MARY. Business or none?

BRODIE. Business or none, little sister! I'll make time, I promise you; and there's another kiss for surety. Come along. (They proceed to push out the chair, L.C.) The wine and wisdom of this evening have given me one of my headaches, and I'm in haste for bed. You'll be good, won't you, and see they make no noise, and let me sleep my fill to-morrow morning till I wake?

MARY. Poor Will! How selfish I must have seemed! You should have told me sooner, and I wouldn't have worried you. Come along.

(She goes out, pushing chair.)

SCENE IX

BRODIE

(He closes, locks, and double-bolts both doors)

BRODIE. Now for one of the Deacon's headaches! Rogues all, rogues all! (Goes to clothes-press, and proceeds to change his coat.) On with the new coat and into the new life! Down with the Deacon and up with the robber! (Changing neck-band and ruffles.) Eh God! how still the house is! There's something in hypocrisy after all. If we were as good as we seem, what would the world be? [The city has its vizard on, and we—at night we are our naked selves. Trysts are keeping, bottles cracking, knives are stripping; and here is Deacon Brodie flaming forth the man of men he is!]—How still it is! . . . My father and Mary—Well! the day for them, the night for me; the grimy cynical night that makes all cats grey, and all honesties of one complexion. Shall a man not have half a life of his own?—not eight hours out of twenty-four? [Eight shall he have should he dare the pit of Tophet.] (Takes out money.) Where's the blunt? I must be cool to-night, or . . . steady, Deacon, you must win; damn you, you must! You must win back the dowry that you've stolen, and marry your sister, and pay your debts, and gull the world a little longer! (As he blows out the lights.) The Deacon's going to bed—the poor sick Deacon! Allons! (Throws up the window, and looks out.) Only the stars to see me! (Addressing the bed.) Lie there, Deacon! sleep and be well to-morrow. As for me, I'm a man once more till morning. (Gets out of the window.)

TABLEAU II. HUNT THE RUNNER

The Scene represents the Procurator's Office.

SCENE I

LAWSON, HUNT

[LAWSON (entering). Step your ways in, Officer. (At wing.) Mr. Carfrae, give a chair to yon decent wife that cam' in wi' me. Nae news?

A VOICE WITHOUT. Naething, sir.

LAWSON (sitting). Weel, Officer, and what can I do for you?]

HUNT. Well, sir, as I was saying, I've an English warrant for the apprehension of one Jemmy Rivers, alias Captain Starlight, now at large within your jurisdiction.

LAWSON. That'll be the highwayman?

HUNT. That same, Mr. Procurator-Fiscal. The Captain's given me a hard hunt of it this time. I dropped on his marks first at Huntingdon, but he was away North, and I had to up and after him. I heard of him all along the York road, for he's a light hand on the pad, has Jemmy, and leaves his mark. [I missed him at York by four-and-twenty hours, and lost him for as much more. Then I picked him up again at Carlisle, and we made a race of it for the Border; but he'd a better nag, and was best up in the road; so I had to wait till I ran him to earth in Edinburgh here and could get a new warrant.] So here I am, sir. They told me you were an active sort of gentleman, and I'm an active man myself.

And Sir John Fielding, Mr. Procurator-Fiscal, he's an active gentleman, likewise, though he's blind as a himage, and he desired his compliments to you, [sir, and said that between us he thought wo'd do the trick].

LAWSON. Ay, he'll be a fine man, Sir John. Hand me owre your papers, Hunt, and you'll have your new warrant quam primum. And see here, Hunt, ye'll aiblins have a while to yoursel', and an active man, as ye say ye are, should aye be grinding grist. We're sair forfeuchen wi' our burglaries. Non constat de personâ. We canna get a grip o' the delinquents. Here is the Hue and Cry. Ye see there is a guid two hundred pounds for ye.

HUNT. Well, Mr. Procurator-Fiscal [I ain't a rich man, and two hundred's two hundred. Thereby, sir], I don't mind telling you I've had a bit of a worry at it already. You see, Mr. Procurator-Fiscal, I had to look into a ken to-night about the Captain, and an old cock always likes to be sure of his walk; so I got one of your Scotch officers—him as was so polite as to show me round to Mr. Brodie's—to give me full particulars about the 'ouse, and the flash companions that use it. In his list I drop on the names of two old lambs of my own; and I put it to you, Mr. Procurator-Fiscal, as a genleman as knows the world, if what's a black sheep in London is likely or not to be keeping school in Edinburgh?

LAWSON. Coelum non animum. A just observe.

HUNT. I'll give it a thought, sir, and see if I can't kill two birds with one stone. Talking of which, Mr. Procurator-Fiscal, I'd like to have a bit of a confab with that nice young woman as came to pay her rent.

LAWSON. Hunt, that's a very decent woman.

HUNT. And a very decent woman may have mighty queer pals, Mr. Procurator-Fiscal. Lord love you, sir, I don't know what the profession would do without 'em!

LAWSON. Ye're vera richt, Hunt. An active and a watchful officer. I'll send her in till ye.

SCENE II

HUNT (solus)

Two hundred pounds reward. Curious thing. One burglary after another, and these Scotch blockheads without a man to show for it. Jock runs east, and Sawney cuts west; everything's at a deadlock; and they go on calling themselves thief-catchers! [By jingo, I'll show them how we do it down South! Well, I've worn out a good deal of saddle leather over Jemmy Rivers; but here's for new breeches if you like.] Let's have another queer at the list. (Reads.) 'Humphrey Moore, otherwise Badger; aged forty, thick-set, dark, close-cropped; has been a prize-fighter; no apparent occupation.' Badger's an old friend of mine, 'George Smith, otherwise the Dook, otherwise Jingling Geordie; red-haired and curly, slight, flash; an old thimble-rig; has been a stroller; suspected of smuggling; an associate of loose women.' G. S., Esquire, is another of my flock. 'Andrew Ainslie, otherwise Slink Ainslie; aged thirty-five; thin, white-faced, lank-haired; no occupation; has been in trouble for reset of theft and subornation of youth; might be useful as king's evidence.' That's an acquaintance to make. 'Jock Hamilton, otherwise Sweepie,' and so on. ['Willie M'Glashan,' hum—yes, and so on, and so on.] Ha! here's the man I want. 'William Brodie, Deacon of the Wrights, about thirty; tall, slim, dark; wears his own hair; is often at Clarke's, but seemingly for purposes of amusement only; [is nephew to the Procurator-Fiscal; is commercially sound, but has of late (it is supposed) been short of cash; has lost much at cock-fighting;] is proud, clever, of good repute, but is fond of adventures and secrecy, and keeps low company.' Now, here's what I ask myself: here's this list of the family party that drop into Mother Clarke's; it's been in the hands of these nincompoops for weeks, and I'm the first to cry Queer Street! Two well-known cracksmen, Badger and the Dook! why, there's Jack in the Orchard at once. This here topsawyer work they talk about, of course that's a chalk above Badger and the Dook. But how about our Mohock-tradesman? 'Purposes of amusement!' What next? Deacon of the Wrights? and wright in their damned lingo means a kind of carpenter, I fancy? Why, damme, it's the man's trade! I'll look you up, Mr. William Brodie, Deacon of the Wrights. As sure as my name's Jerry Hunt, I wouldn't take one-ninety-nine in gold for my chance of that 'ere two hundred!

SCENE III

HUNT; to him JEAN

HUNT. Well, my dear, and how about your gentleman friend now? How about Deacon Brodie?

JEAN. I dinna ken your name, sir, nor yet whae ye are; but this is a very poor employ for ony gentleman—it sets ill wi' ony gentleman to cast my shame in my teeth.

HUNT. Lord love you, my dear, that ain't my line of country. Suppose you're not married and churched a hundred thousand times, what odds to Jerry Hunt? Jerry, my Pamela Prue, is a cove as might be your parent; a cove renowned for the ladies' friend [and he's dead certain to be on your side]. What I can't get over is this: here's this Mr. Deacon Brodie doing the genteel at home, and leaving a nice young 'oman like you—as a cove may say—to take it out on cold potatoes. That's what I can't get over, Mrs. Watt. I'm a family man myself; and I can't get over it.

JEAN. And whae said that to ye? They lee'd whatever. I get naething but guid by him; and I had nae richt to gang to his house; and O, I just ken I've been the ruin of him!

HUNT. Don't you take on, Mrs. Watt. Why, now I hear you piping up for him, I begin to think a lot of him myself. I like a cove to be open-handed and free.

JEAN. Weel, sir, and he's a' that.

HUNT. Well, that shows what a wicked world this is. Why, they told me—. Well, well, 'here's the open 'and and the 'appy 'art.' And how much, my dear—speaking as a family man—now, how much might your gentleman friend stand you in the course of a year?

JEAN. What's your wull?

HUNT. That's a mighty fancy shawl, Mrs. Watt. [I should like to take its next-door neighbour to Mrs. Hunt in King Street, Common Garden.] What's about the figure?

JEAN. It's paid for. Ye can sweir to that.

HUNT. Yes, my dear, and so is King George's crown; but I don't know what it cost, and I don't know where the blunt came from to pay for it.

JEAN. I'm thinking ye'll be a vera clever gentleman.

HUNT. So I am, my dear; and I like you none the worse for being artful yourself. But between friends now, and speaking as a family man—

JEAN. I'll be wishin' ye a fine nicht. (Curtsies and goes out.)

SCENE IV

HUNT (solus)

HUNT. Ah! that's it, is it? 'My fancy man's my 'ole delight,' as we say in Bow Street. But which is the fancy man? George the Dock, or William the Deacon? One or both? (He winks solemnly.) Well, Jerry, my boy, here's your work cut out for you; but if you took one-nine-five for that 'ere little two hundred you'd be a disgrace to the profession.

TABLEAU III. MOTHER CLARKE'S

SCENE I

The Stage represents a room of coarse and sordid appearance: settles, spittoons, etc.; sanded floor. A large table at back, where AINSLIE, HAMILTON, and others are playing cards and quarrelling. In front, L. and R. smaller tables, at one of which are BRODIE and MOORE, drinking. MRS. CLARKE and women serving.

MOORE. You've got the devil's own luck, Deacon, that's what you've got.

BRODIE. Luck! Don't talk of luck to a man like me! Why not say I've the devil's own judgment? Men of my stamp don't risk—they plan, Badger; they plan, and leave chance to such cattle as you [and Jingling Geordie. They make opportunities before they take them].

MOORE. You're artful, ain't you?

BRODIE. Should I be here else? When I leave my house I leave an alibi behind me. I'm ill—ill with a jumping headache, and the fiend's own temper. I'm sick in bed this minute, and they're all going about with the fear of death on them lest they should disturb the poor sick Deacon. [My bedroom door is barred and bolted like the bank—you remember!—and all the while the window's open, and the Deacon's over the hills and far away. What do you think of me?]

MOORE. I've seen your sort before, I have.

BRODIE. Not you. As for Leslie's—

MOORE. That was a nick above you.

BRODIE. Ay was it. He wellnigh took me red-handed; and that was better luck than I deserved. If I'd not been drunk, and in my tantrums, you'd never have got my hand within a thousand years of such a job.

MOORE. Why not? You're the King of the Cracksmen, ain't you?

BRODIE. Why not! He asks me why not! Gods, what a brain it is! Hark ye, Badger, it's all very well to be King of the Cracksmen, as you call it; but however respectable he may have the misfortune to be, one's friend is one's friend, and as such must be severely let alone. What! shall there be no more honour among thieves than there is honesty among politicians? Why, man, if under heaven there were but one poor lock unpicked, and that the lock of one whose claret you've drunk, and who has babbled of woman across your own mahogany—that lock, sir, were entirely sacred. Sacred as the Kirk of Scotland; sacred as King George upon his throne; sacred as the memory of Bruce and Bannockburn.

MOORE. Oh, rot! I ain't a parson, I ain't; I never had no college education. Business is business. That's wot's the matter with me.

BRODIE. Ay, so we said when you lost that fight with Newcastle Jemmy, and sent us all home poor men. That was a nick above you.

MOORE. Newcastle Jemmy! Muck: that's my opinion of him: muck. I'll mop the floor up with him any day, if so be as you or any on 'em 'll make it worth my while. If not, muck! That's my motto. Wot I now ses is, about that 'ere crib at Leslie's, wos I right, I ses? or wos I wrong? That's wot's the matter with you.

BRODIE. You are both right and wrong. You dared me to do it. I was drunk; I was upon my mettle; and I as good as did it. More than that, black-guardly as it was, I enjoyed the doing. He is my friend. He had dined with me that day, and I felt like a man in a story. I climbed his wall, I crawled along his pantry roof, I mounted his window-sill. That one turn of my wrist—you know it I—and the casement was open. It was as dark as the pit, and I thought I'd won my wager, when, phewt! down went something inside, and down went somebody with it. I made one leap, and was off like a rocket. It was my poor friend in person; and if he'd caught and passed me on to the watchman under the window, I should have felt no viler rogue than I feel just now.

MOORE. I s'pose he knows you pretty well by this time?

BRODIE. 'Tis the worst of friendship. Here, Kirsty, fill these glasses. Moore, here's better luck—and a more honourable plant!—next time.

MOORE. Deacon, I looks towards you. But it looks thundering like rotten eggs, don't it?

BRODIE. I think not. I was masked, for one thing, and for another I was as quick as lightning. He suspects me so little that he dined with me this very afternoon.

MOORE. Anyway, you ain't game to try it on again, I'll lay odds on that. Once bit, twice shy. That's your motto.

BRODIE. Right again. I'll put my alibi to a better use. And, Badger, one word in your ear: there's no Newcastle Jemmy about me. Drop the subject, and for good, or I shall drop you. (He rises, and walks backwards and forwards, a little unsteadily. Then returns, and sits L., as before.)

SCENE II

To these, HUNT, disguised

He is disguised as a 'flying stationer' with a patch over his eye. He sits at table opposite BRODIE'S and is served with bread and cheese and beer.

HAMILTON (from behind). The deevil tak' the cairts!

AINSLIE. Hoot, man, dinna blame the cairts.

MOORE. Look here, Deacon, I mean business, I do. (HUNT looks up at the name of 'Deacon.')

BRODIE. Gad, Badger, I never meet you that you do not. [You have a set of the most commercial intentions!] You make me blush.

MOORE. That's all blazing fine, that is! But wot I ses is, wot about the chips? That's what I ses. I'm after that thundering old Excise Office, I am. That's my motto.

BRODIE. 'Tis a very good motto, and at your lips, Badger, it kind of warms my heart. But it's not mine.

MOORE. Muck! why not?

BRODIE. 'Tis too big and too dangerous. I shirk King George; he has a fat pocket, but he has a long arm. [You pilfer sixpence from him, and it's three hundred reward for you, and a hue and cry from Tophet to the stars.] It ceases to be business; it turns politics, and I'm not a politician, Mr. Moore. (Rising.) I'm only Deacon Brodie.

MOORE. All right. I can wait.

BRODIE (seeing HUNT). Ha, a new face,—and with a patch! [There's nothing under heaven I like so dearly as a new face with a patch.] Who the devil, sir, are you that own it? And where did you get it? And how much will you take for it second-hand?

HUNT. Well, sir, to tell you the truth (BRODIE bows) it's not for sale. But it's my own, and I'll drink your honour's health in anything.

BRODIE. An Englishman, too! Badger, behold a countryman. What are you, and what part of southern Scotland do you come from?

HUNT. Well, your honour, to tell you the honest truth—

[BRODIE (bowing). Your obleeged!]

HUNT. I knows a gentleman when I sees him, your honour [and, to tell your honour the truth—

BRODIE. Je vous baise les mains! (Bowing.)]

HUNT. A gentleman as is a gentleman, your honour [is always a gentleman, and to tell you the honest truth]—

BRODIE. Great heavens! answer in three words, and be hanged to you! What are you, and where are you from?

HUNT. A patter-cove from Seven Dials.

BRODIE. Is it possible? All my life long have I been pining to meet with a patter-cove from Seven Dials! Embrace me, at a distance. [A patter-cove from Seven Dials!] Go, fill yourself as drunk as you dare, at my expense. Anything he likes, Mrs. Clarke. He's a patter-cove from Seven Dials. Hillo! what's all this?

AINSLIE. Dod, I'm for nae mair! (At back, and rising.)

PLAYERS. Sit down, Ainslie.—Sit down, Andra.—Ma revenge!

AINSLIE. Na, na, I'm for canny goin'. (Coming forward with bottle.) Deacon, let's see your gless.

BRODIE. Not an inch of it.

MOORE. No rotten shirking, Deacon!

[AINSLIE. I'm sayin', man, let's see your gless.

BRODIE. Go to the deuce!]

AINSLIE. But I'm sayin'—

BRODIE. Haven't I to play to-night?

AINSLIE. But, man, ye'll drink to bonnie Jean Watt?

BRODIE. Ay, I'll follow you there. A la reine de mes amours! (Drinks.) What fiend put this in your way, you hound? You've filled me with raw stuff. By the muckle deil!—

MOORE. Don't hit him, Deacon; tell his mother.

HUNT (aside). Oho!

SCENE III

To these, SMITH, RIVERS.

SMITH. Where's my beloved? Deakin, my beauty, where are you? Come to the arms of George, and let him introduce you. Capting Starlight Rivers! Capting, the Deakin: Deakin, the Capting. An English nobleman on the grand tour, to open his mind, by the Lard!

RIVERS. Stupendiously pleased to make your acquaintance, Mr. Deakin, split me!

[BRODIE. We don't often see England's heroes our way, Captain, but when we do, we make them infernally welcome.

RIVERS. Prettily put, sink me! A demned genteel sentiment, stap my vitals!]

BRODIE. Oh Captain! you flatter me. [We Scotsmen have our qualities, I suppose, but we are but rough and ready at the best. There's nothing like your Englishman for genuine distinction. He is nearer France than we are, and smells of his neighbourhood. That d—d thing, the je ne sais quoi, too! Lard, Lard, split me! stap my vitals! O such manners are pure, pure, pure. They are, by the shade of Claude Duval!]

RIVERS. Mr. Deakin, Mr. Deakin [this is passatively too much]. What will you sip? Give it the hanar of a neam.

BRODIE. By these most hanarable hands now, Captain, you shall not. On such an occasion I could play host with Lucifer himself. Here, Clarke, Mother Midnight! Down with you, Captain! (forcing him boisterously into a chair.) I don't know if you can lie, but, sink me! you shall sit. (Drinking, etc., in dumb-show.)

MOORE (aside to SMITH). We've nobbled him, Geordie!

SMITH (aside to MOORE). As neat as ninepence! He's taking it down like mother's milk. But there'll be wigs on the green to-morrow, Badger! It'll be tuppence and toddle with George Smith.

MOORE. O muck! Who's afraid of him? (To AINSLIE.) Hang on, Slinkie.

HUNT (who is feigning drunkenness, and has overheard; aside). By jingo!

[RIVERS. Will you sneeze, Mr. Deakin, sir?

BRODIE. Thanks; I have all the vices, Captain. You must send me some of your rappee. It is passatively perfect.]

RIVERS. Mr. Deakin, I do myself the hanar of a sip to you.

BRODIE. Topsy-turvy with the can!

MOORE (aside to SMITH). That made him wink.

BRODIE. Your high and mighty hand, my Captain! Shall we dice—dice—dice? (Dumb-show between them.)

AINSLIE (aside to MOORE). I'm sayin'—?

MOORE. What's up now?

AINSLIE. I'm no to gie him the coggit dice?

MOORE. The square ones, rot you! Ain't he got to lose every brass farden?

AINSLIE. What'll like be my share?

MOORE. You mucking well leave that to me.

RIVERS. Well, Mr. Deakin, if you passatively will have me shake a helbow—

BRODIE. Where are the bones, Ainslie? Where are the dice, Lord George? (AINSLIE gives the dice and dice-box to BRODIE; and privately a second pair of dice.) Old Fortune's counters the bonnie money-catching, money-breeding bones! Hark to their dry music! Scotland against England! Sit round, you tame devils, and put your coins on me!

SMITH. Easy does it, my lord of high degree! Keep cool.

BRODIE. Cool's the word, Captain—a cool twenty on the first?

RIVERS. Done and done. (They play.)

HUNT (aside to MOORE, a little drunk). Ain't that 'ere Scotch gentleman, your friend, too drunk to play, sir?

MOORE. You hold your jaw; that's what's the matter with you.

AINSLIE. He's waur nor he looks. He's knockit the box aff the table.

SMITH (picking up box). That's the way we does it. Ten to one and no takers!

BRODIE. Deuces again! More liquor, Mother Clarke!

SMITH. Hooray our side! (Pouting out.) George and his pal for ever!

BRODIE. Deuces again, by heaven! Another?

RIVERS. Done!

BRODIE. Ten more; money's made to go. On with you!

RIVERS. Sixes.

BRODIE. Deuce-ace. Death and judgment? Double or quits?

RIVERS. Drive on! Sixes.

SMITH. Fire away, brave boys! (To MOORE) It's Tally-ho-the-Grinder, Hump!

BRODIE. Treys! Death and the pit! How much have you got there?

RIVERS. A cool forty-five.

BRODIE. I play you thrice the lot.

RIVERS. Who's afraid?

SMITH. Stand by, Badger!

RIVERS. Cinq-ace.

BRODIE. My turn now. (He juggles in and uses the second pair of dice.) Aces! Aces again! What's this? (Picking up dice.) Sold! . . . You play false, you hound!

RIVERS. You lie!

BRODIE. In your teeth. (Overturns table, and goes for him.)

MOORE. Here, none o' that. (They hold him back. Struggle.)

SMITH. Hold on, Deacon!

BRODIE. Let me go. Hands off, I say! I'll not touch him. (Stands weighing dice in his hand.) But as for that thieving whinger, Ainslie, I'll cut his throat between this dark and to-morrow's. To the bone. (Addressing the company.) Rogues, rogues, rogues! (Singing without.) Ha! what's that?

AINSLIE. It's the psalm-singing up by at the Holy Weaver's. And O Deacon, if ye're a Christian man—

THE PSALM WITHOUT:—

'Lord, who shall stand, if Thou, O Lord,
Should'st mark iniquity?
But yet with Thee forgiveness is,
That feared Thou may'st be.'

BRODIE. I think I'll go. 'My son the Deacon was aye regular at kirk.' If the old man could see his son, the Deacon! I think I'll—Ay, who shall stand? There's the rub! And forgiveness, too? There's a long word for you! I learnt it all lang syne, and now . . . hell and ruin are on either hand of me, and the devil has me by the leg. 'My son, the Deacon . . . !' Eh, God! but there's no fool like an old fool! (Becoming conscious of the others.) Rogues!

SMITH. Take my arm, Deacon.

BRODIE. Down, dog, down! [Stay and be drunk with your equals.] Gentlemen and ladies, I have already cursed you pretty heavily. Let me do myself the pleasure of wishing you—a very—good evening. (As he goes out, HUNT, who has been staggering about in the crowd, falls on a settle, as about to sleep.)

ACT - CURTAIN DROP.

ACT II.

TABLEAU IV. EVIL AND GOOD

The Stage represents the Deacon's workshop; benches, shavings, tools, boards, and so forth. Doors, C. on the street, and L. into the house. Without, church bells; not a chime, but a slow broken tocsin.

SCENE I

BRODIE (solus). My head! my head! It's the sickness of the grave. And those bells go on . . . go on! . . . inexorable as death and judgment. [There they go; the trumpets of respectability, sounding encouragement to the world to do and spare not, and not to be found out. Found out! And to those who are they toll as when a man goes to the gallows.] Turn where I will are pitfalls hell-deep. Mary and her dowry; Jean and her child—my child; the dirty scoundrel Moore; my uncle and his trust; perhaps the man from Bow Street. Debt, vice, cruelty, dishonour, crime; the whole canting, lying, double-dealing, beastly business! 'My son the Deacon—Deacon of the Wrights!' My thoughts sicken at it. [Oh the Deacon, the Deacon! Where's a hat for the Deacon? where's a hat for the Deacon's headache? (searching). This place is a piggery. To be respectable and not to find one's hat.)

SCENE II

To him, JEAN, a baby in her shawl. C.

JEAN (who has entered silently during the Deacon's last words). It's me, Wullie.

BRODIE (turning upon her). What! You here again? [you again!]

JEAN. Deacon, I'm unco vexed.

BRODIE. Do you know what you do? Do you know what you risk? [Is there nothing—nothing!—will make you spare me this idiotic, wanton prosecution?]

JEAN. I was wrong to come yestreen; I ken that fine. But the day it's different; I but to come the day, Deacon, though I ken fine it's the Sabbath, and I think shame to be seen upon the streets.

BRODIE. See here, Jean. You must go now. I come to you to-night; I swear that. But now I'm for the road.

JEAN. No till you've heard me, William Brodie. Do ye think I came to pleasure mysel', where I'm no wanted? I've a pride o' my ains.

BRODIE. Jean, I am going now. If you please to stay on alone, in this house of mine, where I wish I could say you are welcome, stay (going).

JEAN. It's the man frae Bow Street.

BRODIE. Bow Street?

JEAN. I thocht ye would hear me. Ye think little o' me; but it's mebbe a braw thing for you that I think sae muckle o' William Brodie . . . ill as it sets me.

BRODIE. [You don't know what is on my mind, Jeannie, else you would forgive me.] Bow Street?

JEAN. It's the man Hunt: him that was here yestreen for the Fiscal.

BRODIE. Hunt?

JEAN. He kens a hantle. He . . . Ye maunna be angered wi' me, Wullie! I said what I shouldna.

BRODIE. Said? Said what?

JEAN. Just that ye were a guid frien' to me. He made believe he was awful sorry for me, because ye gied me nae siller; and I said, 'Wha tellt him that?' and that he lee'd.

BRODIE. God knows he did! What next?

JEAN. He was that soft-spoken, butter wouldna melt in his mouth; and he keepit aye harp, harpin'; but after that let out, he got neither black nor white frae me. Just that ae word and nae mair; and at the hinder end he just speired straucht out, whaur it was ye got your siller frae.

BRODIE. Where I got my siller?

JEAN. Ay, that was it! 'You ken,' says he.

BRODIE. Did he? and what said you?

JEAN. I couldna think on naething, but just that he was a gey and clever gentleman.

BRODIE. You should have said I was in trade, and had a good business. That's what you should have said. That's what you would have said had you been worth your salt. But it's blunder, blunder, outside and in [upstairs, downstairs, and in my lady's chamber]. You women! Did he see Smith?

JEAN. Ay, and kennt him.

BRODIE. Damnation!—No, I'm not angry with you. But you see what I've to endure for you. Don't cry. [Here's the devil at the door, and we must bar him out as best we can.]

JEAN. God's truth, ye are nae vexed wi' me?

BRODIE. God's truth, I am grateful to you. How is the child? Well? That's right. (Peeping.) Poor wee laddie! He's like you, Jean.

JEAN. I aye thocht he was liker you.

BRODIE. Is he? Perhaps he is. Ah, Jeannie, you must see and make him a better man than his father.

JEAN. Eh man, Deacon, the proud wumman I'll be gin he's only half sae guid.

BRODIE. Well, well, if I win through this, we'll see what we can do for him between us. (Leading her out, C.) And now, go—go—go.

LAWSON (without, L.). I ken the way, I ken the way.

JEAN (starring to door). It's the Fiscal; I'm awa. (BRODIE, L.).

SCENE III

To these, LAWSON, L.

LAWSON. A braw day this, William. (Seeing JEAN.) Eh Mistress Watt? And what'll have brocht you here?

BRODIE (seated on bench). Something, uncle, she lost last night, and she thinks that something she lost is here. Voilà.

LAWSON. Why are ye no at the kirk, woman? Do ye gang to the kirk?

JEAN. I'm mebbe no what ye would just ca' reg'lar. Ye see, Fiscal, it's the wean.

LAWSON. A bairn's an excuse; I ken that fine, Mistress Watt. But bairn or nane, my woman, ye should be at the kirk. Awa wi' ye! Hear to the bells; they're ringing in. (JEAN curtsies to both, and goes out C. The bells which have been ringing quicker, cease.)

SCENE IV

LAWSON (to BRODIE, returning C. from door). Mulier formosa superne, William: a braw lass, and a decent woman forbye.

BRODIE. I'm no judge, Procurator, but I'll take your word for it. Is she not a tenant of yours?

LAWSON. Ay, ay; a bit house on my land in Liberton's Wynd. Her man's awa, puir body; or they tell me sae; and I'm concerned for her [she's unco bonnie to be left her lane]. But it sets me brawly to be finding faut wi' the puir lass, and me an elder, and should be at the plate. [There'll be twa words about this in the Kirk Session.] However, it's nane of my business that brings me, or I should tak' the mair shame to mysel'. Na, sir, it's for you; it's your business keeps me frae the kirk.

BRODIE. My business, Procurator? I rejoice to see it in such excellent hands.

LAWSON. Ye see, it's this way. I had a crack wi' the laddie, Leslie, inter pocula (he took a stirrup-cup wi' me), and he tells me he has askit Mary, and she was to speak to ye hersel'. O, ye needna look sae gash. Did she speak? and what'll you have said to her?

BRODIE. She has not spoken; I have said nothing; and I believe I asked you to avoid the subject.

LAWSON. Ay, I made a note o' that observation, William [and assoilzied mysel']. Mary's a guid lass, and I'm her uncle, and I'm here to be answered. Is it to be ay or no?

BRODIE. It's to be no. This marriage must be quashed; and hark ye, Procurator, you must help me.

LAWSON. Me? ye're daft! And what for why?

BRODIE. Because I've spent the trust-money, and I can't refund it.

LAWSON. Ye reprobate deevil!

BRODIE. Have a care, Procurator. No wry words!

LAWSON. Do you say it to my face, sir? Dod, sir, I'm the Crown Prosecutor.

BRODIE. Right. The Prosecutor for the Crown. And where did you get your brandy?

LAWSON. Eh?

BRODIE. Your brandy! Your brandy man! Where do you get your brandy? And you a Crown official and an elder!

LAWSON. Whaur the deevil did ye hear that?

BRODIE. Rogues all! Rogues all, Procurator!

LAWSON. Ay, ay. Lord save us! Guidsake, to think o' that noo! . . . Can ye give me some o' that Cognac? I'm . . . I'm sort o' shaken, William, I'm sort o' shaken. Thank you, William! (Looking, piteously at glass.) Nunc est bibendum. (Drinks.) Troth, I'm set ajee a bit. Wha the deevil tauld ye?

BRODIE. Ask no questions, brother. We are a pair.

LAWSON. Pair, indeed! Pair, William Brodie! Upon my saul, sir, ye're a brazen-faced man that durst say it to my face! Tak' you care, my bonnie young man, that your craig doesna feel the wecht o' your hurdies. Keep the plainstanes side o' the gallows. Via trita, via tuta, William Brodie!

BRODIE. And the brandy, Procurator? and the brandy?

LAWSON. Ay . . . weel . . . be't sae! Let the brandy bide, man, let the brandy bide! But for you and the trust-money . . . damned! It's felony. Tutor in rem suam, ye ken, tutor in rem suam. But O man, Deacon, whaur is the siller?

BRODIE. It's gone—O how the devil should I know? But it'll never come back.

LAWSON. Dear, dear! A' gone to the winds o' heaven! Sae ye're an extravagant dog, too. Prodigus et furiosus! And that puir lass—eh, Deacon, man, that puir lass! I mind her such a bonny bairn.

BRODIE (stopping his ears). Brandy, brandy, brandy, brandy, brandy

LAWSON. William Brodie, mony's the long day that I've believed in you; prood, prood was I to be the Deacon's uncle; and a sore hearing have I had of it the day. That's past; that's past like Flodden Field; it's an auld sang noo, and I'm an aulder man than when I crossed your door. But mark ye this—mark ye this, William Brodie, I may be no sae guid's I should be; but there's no a saul between the east sea and the wast can lift his een to God that made him, and say I wranged him as ye wrang that lassie. I bless God, William Brodie—ay, though he was like my brother—I bless God that he that got ye has the hand of death upon his hearing, and can win into his grave a happier man than me. And ye speak to me, sir? Think shame—think shame upon your heart!

BRODIE. Rogues all!

LAWSON. You're the son of my sister, William Brodie. Mair than that I stop not to inquire. If the siller is spent, and the honour tint—Lord help us, and the honour tint!—sae be it, I maun bow the head. Nuin shall... come by me. Na, and I'll say mair, William; we have a' our weary sins upon our backs, and maybe I have mair than mony. But, man, if ye could bring half the jointure . . . [potius quam pereas] . . . for your mither's son? Na? You couldna bring the half? Weel, weel, it's a sair heart I have this day, a sair heart and a weary. If I were a better man mysel' . . . but there, there, it's a sair heart that I have gotten. And the Lord kens I'll help ye if I can. [Potius quam pereas.]

SCENE V

BRODIE. Sore hearing, does he say? My hand's wet. But it's victory. Shall it be go? or stay? [I should show them all I can, or they may pry closer than they ought.] Shall I have it out and be done with it? To see Mary at once [to carry bastion after bastion at the charge]—there were the true safety after all! Hurry—hurry's the road to silence now. Let them once get tattling in their parlours, and it's death to me. For I'm in a cruel corner now. I'm down, and I shall get my kicking soon and soon enough. I began it in the lust of life, in a hey-day of mystery and adventure. I felt it great to be a bolder, craftier rogue than the drowsy citizen that called himself my fellow-man. [It was meat and drink to know him in the hollow of my hand, hoarding that I and mine might squander, pinching that we might wax fat.] It was in the laughter of my heart that I tip-toed into his greasy privacy. I forced the strong-box at his ear while he sprawled beside his wife. He was my butt, my ape, my jumping-jack. And now . . . O fool, fool! [Duped by such knaves as are a shame to knavery, crime's rabble, hell's tatterdemalions!] Shorn to the quick! Rooked to my vitals! And I must thieve for my daily bread like any crawling blackguard in the gutter. And my sister . . . my kind, innocent sister! She will come smiling to me with her poor little love-story, and I must break her heart. Broken hearts, broken lives! . . . I should have died before.

SCENE VI

BRODIE, MARY

MARY (tapping without). Can I come in, Will?

BRODIE. O yes, come in, come in! (MARY enters.) I wanted to be quiet, but it doesn't matter, I see. You women are all the same.

MARY. O no, Will, they're not all so happy, and they're not all Brodies. But I'll be a woman in one thing. For I've come to claim your promise, dear; and I'm going to be petted and comforted and made much of, altho' I don't need it, and . . . Why, Will, what's wrong with you? You look . . . I don't know what you look like.

BRODIE. O nothing! A splitting head and an aching heart. Well! you've come to speak to me. Speak up. What is it? Come, girl! What is it? Can't you speak?

MARY. Why, Will, what is the matter?

BRODIE. I thought you had come to tell me something. Here I am. For God's sake out with it, and don't stand beating about the bush.

MARY. O be kind, be kind to me.

BRODIE. Kind? I am kind. I'm only ill and worried, can't you see? Whimpering? I knew it! Sit down, you goose! Where do you women get your tears?

MARY. Why are you so cross with me? Oh, Will, you have forgot your sister! Remember, dear, that I have nobody but you. It's your own fault, Will, if you've taught me to come to you for kindness, for I always found it. And I mean you shall be kind to me again. I know you will, for this is my great need, and the day I've missed my mother sorest. Just a nice look, dear, and a soft tone in your voice, to give me courage, for I can tell you nothing till I know that you're my own brother once again.

BRODIE. If you'd take a hint, you'd put it off till to-morrow. But I suppose you won't. On, then, I'm listening. I'm listening!

MARY. Mr. Leslie has asked me to be his wife.

BRODIE. He has, has he?

MARY. And I have consented.

BRODIE. And . . . ?

MARY. You can say that to me? And that is all you have to say?

BRODIE. O no, not all.

MARY. Speak out, sir. I am not afraid.

BRODIE. I suppose you want my consent?

MARY. Can you ask?

BRODIE. I didn't know. You seem to have got on pretty well without it so far.

MARY. O shame on you! shame on you!

BRODIE. Perhaps you may be able to do without it altogether. I hope so. For you'll never have it. . . . Mary! . . . I hate to see you look like that. If I could say anything else, believe me, I would say it. But I have said all; every word is spoken; there's the end.

MARY. It shall not be the end. You owe me explanation; and I'll have it.

BRODIE. Isn't my 'No' enough, Mary?

MARY. It might be enough for me; but it is not, and it cannot be, enough for him. He has asked me to be his wife; he tells me his happiness is in my hands—poor hands, but they shall not fail him, if my poor heart should break! If he has chosen and set his hopes upon me, of all women in the world, I shall find courage somewhere to be worthy of the choice. And I dare you to leave this room until you tell me all your thoughts—until you prove that this is good and right.

BRODIE. Good and right? They are strange words, Mary. I mind the time when it was good and right to be your father's daughter and your brother's sister . . . Now! . . .

MARY. Have I changed? Not even in thought. My father, Walter says, shall live and die with us. He shall only have gained another son. And you—you know what he thinks of you; you know what I would do for you.

BRODIE. Give him up.

MARY. I have told you: not without a reason.

BRODIE. You must.

MARY. I will not.

BRODIE. What if I told you that you could only compass your happiness and his at the price of my ruin?

MARY. Your ruin?

BRODIE. Even so.

MARY. Ruin!

BRODIE. It has an ugly sound, has it not?

MARY. O Willie, what have you done? What have you done? What have you done?

BRODIE. I cannot tell you, Mary. But you may trust me. You must give up this Leslie . . . and at once. It is to save me.

MARY. I would die for you, dear, you know that. But I cannot be false to him. Even for you, I cannot be false to him.

BRODIE. We shall see. Let me take you to your room. Come. And, remember, it is for your brother's sake. It is to save me.

MARY. I am true Brodie. Give me time, and you shall not find me wanting. But it is all so sudden . . . so strange and dreadful! You will give me time, will you not? I am only a woman, and . . . O my poor Walter! It will break his heart! It will break his heart! (A knock.)

BRODIE. You hear!

MARY. Yes, yes. Forgive me. I am going. I will go. It is to save you, is it not? To save you. Walter . . . Mr. Leslie . . . O Deacon, Deacon, God forgive you! (She goes out.)

BRODIE. Amen. But will He?

SCENE VII

BRODIE, HUNT

HUNT (hat in hand). Mr. Deacon Brodie, I believe?

BRODIE. I am he, Mr.—

HUNT. Hunt, sir; an officer from Sir John Fielding of Bow Street.

BRODIE. There can be no better passport than the name. In what can I serve you?

HUNT. You'll excuse me, Mr. Deacon.

BRODIE. Your duty excuses you, Mr. Hunt.

HUNT. Your obedient. The fact is, Mr. Deacon [we in the office see a good deal of the lives of private parties; and I needn't tell a gentleman of your experience it's part of our duty to hold our tongues. Now], it's come to my knowledge that you are a trifle jokieous. Of course I know there ain't any harm in that. I've been young myself, Mr. Deacon, and speaking—

BRODIE. O, but pardon me. Mr. Hunt, I am not going to discuss my private character with you.

HUNT. To be sure you ain't. [And do I blame you? Not me.] But, speaking as one man of the world to another, you naturally see a great deal of bad company.

BRODIE. Not half so much as you do. But I see what you're driving at; and if I can illuminate the course of justice, you may command me. (He sits, and motions HUNT to do likewise.)

HUNT. I was dead sure of it; and 'and upon 'art, Mr. Deacon, I thank you. Now (consulting pocket-book), did you ever meet a certain George Smith?

BRODIE. The fellow they call Jingling Geordie? (HUNT nods.) Yes.

HUNT. Bad character.

BRODIE. Let us say . . . disreputable.

HUNT. Any means of livelihood?

BRODIE. I really cannot pretend to guess, I have met the creature at cock-fights [which, as you know, are my weakness]. Perhaps he bets.

HUNT. [Mr. Deacon, from what I know of the gentleman, I should say that if he don't—if he ain't open to any mortal thing—he ain't the man I mean.] He used to be about with a man called Badger Moore.

BRODIE. The boxer?

HUNT. That's him. Know anything of him?

BRODIE. Not much. I lost five pieces on him in a fight; and I fear he sold his backers.

HUNT. Speaking as one admirer of the noble art to another, Mr. Deacon, the losers always do. I suppose the Badger cockfights like the rest of us?

BRODIE. I have met him in the pit.

HUNT. Well, it's a pretty sport. I'm as partial to a main as anybody.

BRODIE. It's not an elegant taste, Mr. Hunt.

HUNT. It costs as much as though it was. And that reminds me, speaking as one sportsman to another, Mr. Deacon, I was sorry to hear that you've been dropping a hatful of money lately.

BRODIE. You are very good.

HUNT. Four hundred in three months, they tell me.

BRODIE. Ah!

HUNT. So they say, sir.

BRODIE. They have a perfect right to say so, Mr. Hunt.

HUNT. And you to do the other thing? Well, I'm a good hand at keeping close myself.

BRODIE. I am not consulting you, Mr. Hunt; 'tis you who are consulting me. And if there is nothing else (rising) in which I can pretend to serve you . . . ?

HUNT (rising). That's about all, sir, unless you can put me on to anything good in the way of heckle and spur? I'd try to look in.

BRODIE. O, come, Mr. Hunt, if you have nothing to do, frankly and flatly I have. This is not the day for such a conversation; and so good-bye to you. (A knocking, C.)

HUNT. Servant, Mr. Deacon. (SMITH and MOORE, without waiting to be answered, open and enter, C. They are well into the room before they observe HUNT.) [Talk of the Devil, sir!]

BRODIE. What brings you here? (SMITH and MOORE, confounded by the officer's presence, slouch together to right of door. HUNT, stopping as he goes out, contemplates the pair, sarcastically. This is supported by MOORE with sullen bravado; by SMITH, with cringing airiness.)

HUNT (digging SMITH in the ribs). Why, you are the very parties I was looking for! (He goes out, C.)

SCENE VIII

BRODIE, MOORE, SMITH

MOORE. Wot was that cove here about?

BRODIE (with folded arms, half-sitting on bench). He was here about you.

SMITH (still quite discountenanced). About us? Scissors! And what did you tell him?

BRODIE (same attitude). I spoke of you as I have found you. [I told him you were a disreputable hound, and that Moore had crossed a fight.] I told him you were a drunken ass, and Moore an incompetent and dishonest boxer.

MOORE. Look here, Deacon! Wot's up? Wot I ses is, if a cove's got any thundering grudge agin a cove, why can't he spit it out, I ses.

BRODIE. Here are my answers (producing purse and dice). These are both too light. This purse is empty, these dice are not loaded. Is it indiscretion to inquire how you share? Equal with the Captain, I presume?

SMITH. It's as easy as my eye, Deakin. Slink Ainslie got letting the merry glass go round, and didn't know the right bones from the wrong. That's hall.

BRODIE. [What clumsy liars you are!

SMITH. In boyhood's hour, Deakin, he were called Old Truthful. Little did he think—]

BRODIE. What is your errand?

MOORE. Business.

SMITH. After the melancholy games of last night, Deakin, which no one deplores so much as George Smith, we thought we'd trot round—didn't us, Hump? and see how you and your bankers was a-getting on.

BRODIE. Will you tell me your errand?

MOORE. You're dry, ain't you?

BRODIE. Am I?

MOORE. We ain't none of us got a stiver, that's wot's the matter with us.

BRODIE. Is it?

MOORE. Ay, strike me, it is! And wot we've got to is to put up the Excise.

SMITH. It's the last plant in the shrubbery Deakin, and it's breaking George the gardener's heart, it is. We really must!

BRODIE. Must we?

MOORE. Must's the thundering word. I mean business, I do.

BRODIE. That's lucky. I don't.

MOORE. O, you don't, don't you?

BRODIE. I do not.

MOORE. Then p'raps you'll tell us wot you thundering well do?

BRODIE. What do I mean? I mean that you and that merry-andrew shall walk out of this room and this house. Do you suppose, you blockheads, that I am blind? I'm the Deacon, am I not? I've been your king and your commander. I've led you, and fed you, and thought for you with this head. And you think to steal a march upon a man like me? I see you through and through [I know you like the clock]; I read your thoughts like print. Brodie, you thought, has money, and won't do the job. Therefore, you thought, we must rook him to the heart. And therefore, you put up your idiot cockney. And now you come round, and dictate, and think sure of your Excise? Sure? Are you sure I'll let you pack with a whole skin? By my soul, but I've a mind to pistol you like dogs. Out of this! Out, I say, and soil my home no more.

MOORE (sitting). Now look 'ere. Mr. bloody Deacon Brodie, you see this 'ere chair of yours, don't you? Wot I ses to you is, here I am, I ses, and here I mean to stick. That's my motto. Who the devil are you to do the high and mighty? You make all you can out of us, don't you? and when one of your plants get cross, you order us out of the ken? Muck! That's wot I think of you. Muck! Don't you get coming the nob over me, Mr. Deacon Brodie, or I'll smash you.

BRODIE. You will?

MOORE. Ay will I. If I thundering well swing for it. And as for clearing out? Muck! Here I am, and here I stick. Clear out? You try it on. I'm a man, I am.

BRODIE. This is plain speaking.

MOORE. Plain? Wot about your father as can't walk? Wot about your fine-madam sister? Wot about the stone-jug, and the dock, and the rope in the open street? Is that plain? If it ain't, you let me know, and I'll spit it out so as it'll raise the roof off this 'ere ken. Plain! I'm that cove's master, and I'll make it plain enough for him.

BRODIE. What do you want of me?

MOORE. Wot do I want of you? Now you speak sense. Leslie's is wot I want of you. The Excise is wot I want of you. Leslie's to-night and the Excise to-morrow. That's wot I want of you, and wot I thundering well mean to get.

BRODIE. Damn you!

MOORE. Amen. But you've got your orders.

BRODIE (with pistol). Orders? hey? orders?

SMITH (between them). Deacon, Deacon!—Badger, are you mad?

MOORE. Muck! That's my motto. Wot I ses is, has he got his orders or has he not? That's wot's the matter with him.

SMITH. Deacon, half a tick. Humphrey, I'm only a light weight, and you fight at twelve stone ten, but I'm damned if I'm going to stand still and see you hitting a pal when he's down.

MOORE. Muck! That's wot I think of you.

SMITH. He's a cut above us, ain't he? He never sold his backers, did he? We couldn't have done without him, could we? You dry up about his old man, and his sister; and don't go on hitting a pal when he's knocked out of time and cannot hit back, for, damme, I will not stand it.

MOORE. Amen to you. But I'm cock of this here thundering walk, and that cove's got his orders.

BRODIE (putting pistol on bench). I give in. I will do your work for you once more. Leslie's to-night and the Excise to-morrow. If that is enough, if you have no more . . . orders, you may count it as done.

MOORE. Fen larks. No rotten shirking, mind.

BRODIE. I have passed you my word. And now you have said what you came to say, you must go. I have business here; but two hours hence I am at your . . . orders. Where shall I await you?

MOORE. What about that woman's place of yours?

BRODIE. Your will is my law.

MOORE. That's good enough. Now, Dock.

SMITH. Bye-bye, my William. Don't forget.

SCENE IX

BRODIE. Trust me. No man forgets his vice, you dogs, or forgives it either. It must be done: Leslie's to-night and the Excise to-morrow. It shall be done. This settles it. They used to fetch and carry for me, and now . . . I've licked their boots, have I? I'm their man, their tool, their chattel. It's the bottom rung of the ladder of shame. I sound with my foot, and there's nothing underneath but the black emptiness of damnation. Ah, Deacon, Deacon, and so this is where you've been travelling all these years; and it's for this that you learned French! The gallows . . . God help me, it begins to dog me like my shadow. There's a step to take! And the jerk upon your spine! How's a man to die with a night-cap on? I've done with this. Over yonder, across the great ocean, is a new land, with new characters, and perhaps new lives. The sun shines, and the bells ring, and it's a place where men live gladly; and the Deacon himself can walk without terror, and begin again like a new-born child. It must be good to see day again and not to fear; it must be good to be one's self with all men. Happy like a child, wise like a man, free like God's angels . . . should I work these hands off and eat crusts, there were a life to make me young and good again. And it's only over the sea! O man, you have been blind, and now your eyes are opened. It was half a life's nightmare, and now you are awake. Up, Deacon, up, it's hope that's at the window! Mary! Mary! Mary!

SCENE X

BRODIE, MARY, OLD BRODIE

(BRODIE has fallen into a chair, with his face upon the table. Enter MARY, by the side door pushing her father's chair. She is supposed to have advanced far enough for stage purposes before BRODIE is aware of her. He starts up, and runs to her.)

BRODIE. Look up, my lass, look up, and be a woman! I . . . O kiss me, Mary I give me a kiss for my good news.

MARY. Good news, Will? Is it changed?

BRODIE. Changed? Why, the world's a different colour! It was night, and now it's broad day and I trust myself again. You must wait, dear, wait, and I must work and work; and before the week is out, as sure as God sees me, I'll have made you happy. O you may think me broken, hounds, but the Deacon's not the man to be run down; trust him, he shall turn a corner yet, and leave you snarling! And you, Poll, you. I've done nothing for you yet; but, please God, I'll make your life a life of gold; and wherever I am, I'll have a part in your happiness, and you'll know it, by heaven! and bless me.

MARY. O Willie, look at him; I think he hears you, and is trying to be glad with us.

BRODIE. My son—Deacon—better man than I was.

BRODIE. O for God's sake, hear him!

MARY. He is quite happy, Will, and so am I . . . so am I.

BRODIE. Hear me, Mary. This is a big moment in our two lives. I swear to you by the father here between us that it shall not be fault of mine if this thing fails; if this ship founders you have set your hopes in. I swear it by our father; I swear it by God's judgments.

MARY. I want no oaths, Will.

BRODIE. No, but I do. And prayers, Mary, prayers. Pray night and day upon your knees. I must move mountains.

OLD BRODIE. A wise son maketh—maketh—

BRODIE. A glad father? And does your son, the Deacon, make you glad? O heaven of heavens, if I were a good man.

ACT - CURTAIN DROP.

ACT III.

TABLEAU V. KING'S EVIDENCE

The Stage represents a public place in Edinburgh.

SCENE I

JEAN, SMITH, and MOORE

(They loiter in L., and stand looking about as for somebody not there. SMITH is hat in hand to JEAN; MOORE as usual.)

MOORE. Wot did I tell you? Is he 'ere, or ain't he? Now, then. Slink by name and Slink by nature, that's wot's the matter with him.

JEAN. He'll no be lang; he's regular enough, if that was a'.

MOORE. I'd regular him; I'd break his back.

SMITH. Badger, you brute, you hang on to the lessons of your dancing-master. None but the genteel deserves the fair; does they, Duchess?

MOORE. O rot! Did I insult the blowen? Wot's the matter with me is Slink Ainslie.

SMITH. All right, old Crossed-in-love. Give him forty winks, and he'll turn up as fresh as clean sawdust and as respectable as a new Bible.

MOORE. That's right enough; but I ain't agoing to stand here all day for him. I'm for a drop of something short, I am. You tell him I showed you that (showing his doubled fist). That's wot's the matter with him. (He lurches out, R.)

SCENE II

SMITH and JEAN, to whom HUNT, and afterwards MOORE

SMITH (critically). No, Duchess, he has not good manners.

JEAN. Ay, he's an impident man.

SMITH. So he is, Jean; and for the matter of that he ain't the only one.

JEAN. Geordie, I want nae mair o' your nonsense, mind.

SMITH. There's our old particular the Deacon, now. Why is he ashamed of a lovely woman? That's not my idea of the Young Chevalier, Jean. If I had luck, we should be married, and retire to our estates in the country, shouldn't us? and go to church and be happy, like the nobility and gentry.

JEAN. Geordie Smith, div ye mean ye'd mairry me?

SMITH. Mean it? What else has ever been the 'umble petition of your honest but well-meaning friend, Roman, and fellow-countryman? I know the Deacon's your man, and I know he's a cut above G. S.; but he won't last, Jean, and I shall.

JEAN. Ay, I'm muckle ta'en up wi' him; wha could help it?

SMITH. Well, and my sort don't grow on apple-trees either.

JEAN. Ye're a fine, cracky, neebourly body, Geordie, if ye wad just let me be.

SMITH. I know I ain't a Scotchman born

JEAN. I dinna think sae muckle the waur o' ye even for that; if ye would just let me be.

[HUNT (entering behind, aside). Are they thick? Anyhow, it's a second chance.]

SMITH. But he won't last, Jean, and when he leaves you, you come to me. Is that your taste in pastry? That's the kind of harticle that I present.

HUNT (surprising them as in Tableau I.). Why, you're the very parties I was looking for!

JEAN. Mercy me!

SMITH. Damn it, Jerry, this is unkind.

HUNT. [Now this is what I call a picter of good fortune.] Ain't it strange I should have dropped across you comfortable and promiscuous like this?

JEAN (stolidly). I hope ye're middling weel, Mr. Hunt? (Going.) Mr. Smith!

SMITH. Mrs. Watt, ma'am! (Going.)

HUNT. Hold hard, George. Speaking as one lady's man to another, turn about's fair play. You've had your confab, and now I'm going to have mine. [Not that I've done with you; you stand by and wait.] Ladies first, George, ladies first; that's the size of it. (To JEAN, aside.) Now, Mrs. Watt, I take it you ain't a natural fool?

JEAN. And thank ye kindly, Mr. Hunt.

SMITH (interfering). Jean . . . !

HUNT (keeping him off). Half a tick, George. (To JEAN.) Mrs. Watt, I've a warrant in my pocket. One, two, three: will you peach?

JEAN. Whaten kind of a word'll that be?

SMITH. Mum it is, Jean!

HUNT. When you've done dancing, George! (To JEAN.) It ain't a pretty expression, my dear, I own it. 'Will you blow the gaff?' is perhaps more tenderer.

JEAN. I think ye've a real strange way o' expressin yoursel'.

HUNT (to JEAN). I can't waste time on you, my girl. It's now or never. Will you turn king's evidence?

JEAN. I think ye'll have made a mistake, like.

HUNT. Well, I'm . . . ! (Separating them.) [No, not yet; don't push me.] George's turn now. (To GEORGE.) George, I've a warrant in my pocket.

SMITH. As per usual, Jerry?

HUNT. Now I want king's evidence.

SMITH. Ah! so you came a cropper with her, Jerry. Pride had a fall.

HUNT. A free pardon and fifty shiners down.

SMITH. A free pardon, Jerry?

HUNT. Don't I tell you so?

SMITH. And fifty down? fifty?

HUNT. On the nail.

SMITH. So you came a cropper with her, and then you tried it on with me?

HUNT. I suppose you mean you're a born idiot?

SMITH. What I mean is, Jerry, that you've broke my heart. I used to look up to you like a party might to Julius Cæsar. One more of boyhood's dreams gone pop. (Enter MOORE, L.)

HUNT (to both). Come, then, I'll take the pair, and be damned to you. Free pardon to both, fifty down and the Deacon out of the way. I don't care for you commoners, it's the Deacon I want.

JEAN (looking off stolidly). I think the kirks are scalin'. There seems to be mair people in the streets.

HUNT. O that's the way, is it? Do you know that I can hang you, my woman, and your fancy man a well?

JEAN. I daur say ye would like fine, Mr. Hunt; and here's my service to you. (Going.)

HUNT. George, don't you be a tomfool, anyway. Think of the blowen here, and have brains for two.

SMITH (going). Ah, Jerry, if you knew anything, how different you would talk! (They go together, R.)

SCENE III

HUNT, MOORE

HUNT. Half a tick, Badger. You're a man of parts, you are; you're solid, you're a true-born Englishman; you ain't a Jerry-go-Nimble like him. Do you know what your pal the Deacon's worth to you? Fifty golden Georges and a free pardon. No questions asked, and no receipts demanded. What do you say? Is it a deal?

MOORE (as to himself). Muck. (He goes out, R.)

SCENE IV

HUNT, to whom AINSLIE

HUNT (looking after them ruefully). And these were the very parties I was looking for! [Ah, Jerry, Jerry, if they knew this at the office!] Well, the market price of that 'ere two hundred is a trifle on the decline and fall. (Looking L.) Hullo! (Slapping his thigh). Send me victorious! It's king's evidence on two legs. (Advancing with great cordiality to meet AINSLIE, who enters L.) And so your name's Andrew Ainslie, is it? As I was saying, you're the very party I was looking for. Ain't it strange, now, that I should have dropped across you comfortable and promiscuous like this?

AINSLIE. I dinna ken wha ye are, an' I'm ill for my bed.

HUNT. Let your bed wait, Andrew. I want a little chat with you; just a quiet little sociable wheeze. Just about our friends, you know. About Badger Moore, and George the Dook, and Jemmy Rivers, and Deacon Brodie, Andrew. Particularly Deacon Brodie.

AINSLIE. They're nae friens o' mine's, mister. I ken naething an' naebody. An' noo I'll get to my bed, wulln't I?

HUNT. We're going to have our little talk out first. After that perhaps I'll let you go, and perhaps I won't. It all depends on how we get along together. Now, in a general way, Andrew, and speaking of a man as you find him, I'm all for peace and quietness myself. That's my usual game, Andrew, but when I do make a dust I'm considered by my friends to be rather a good hand at it. So don't you tread upon the worm.

AINSLIE. But I'm sayin'—

HUNT. You leave that to me, Andrew. You shall do your pitch presently. I'm first on the ground, and I lead off. With a question, Andrew. Did you ever hear in your life of such a natural curiosity as a Bow Street Runner?

AINSLIE. Aiblins ay an' aiblins no.

HUNT. 'Aiblins ay and aiblins no.' Very good indeed, Andrew. Now, I'll ask you another. Did you ever see a Bow Street Runner, Andrew? With the naked eye, so to speak?

AINSLIE. What's your wull?

HUNT. Artful bird! Now since we're getting on so cosy and so free, I'll ask you another, Andrew. Should you like to see a Bow Street Runner? (Producing staff.) 'Cos, if so, you've only got to cast your eyes on me. Do you queer the red weskit, Andrew? Pretty colour, ain't it? So nice and warm for the winter too. (AINSLIE dives, HUNT collars him.) No, you don't. Not this time. Run away like that before we've finished our little conversation? You're a nice young man, you are. Suppose we introduce our wrists into these here darbies? Now we shall get along cosier and freer than ever. Want to lie down, do you? All right! anything to oblige.

AINSLIE (grovelling). It wasna me, it wasna me. It's bad companions; I've been lost wi' bad companions an' the drink. An' O mister, ye'll be a kind gentleman to a puir lad, an' me sae weak, an' fair rotten wi' the drink an' that. Ye've a bonnie kind heart, my dear, dear gentleman; ye wadna hang sitchan a thing as me. I'm no fit to hang. They ca' me the Cannleworm! An' I'll dae somethin' for ye, wulln't I? An' ye'll can hang the ithers?

HUNT. I thought I hadn't mistook my man. Now, you look here, Andrew Ainslie, you're a bad lot. I've evidence to hang you fifty times over. But the Deacon is my mark. Will you peach, or wont you? You blow the gaff, and I'll pull you through. You don't, and I'll scrag you as sure as my name's Jerry Hunt.

AINSLIE. I'll dae onything. It's the hanging fleys me. I'll dae onything, onything no to hang.

HUNT. Don't lie crawling there, but get up and answer me like a man. Ain't this Deacon Brodie the fine workman that's been doing all these tip-topping burglaries?

AINSLIE. It's him, mister; it's him. That's the man. Ye're in the very bit. Deacon Brodie. I'll can tak' ye to his vera door.

HUNT. How do you know?

AINSLIE. I gi'ed him a han' wi' them a'. It was him an' Badger Moore, and Geordie Smith; an' they gart me gang wi' them whether or no; I'm that weak, an' whiles I'm donner'd wi' the drink. But I ken a', an' I'll tell a'. And O kind gentleman, you'll speak to their lordships for me, an' I'll no be hangit . . . I'll no be hangit, wull I?

HUNT. But you shared, didn't you? I wonder what share they thought you worth. How much did you get for last night's performance down at Mother Clarke's?

AINSLIE. Just five pund, mister. Five pund. As sure's deith it wadna be a penny mair. No but I askit mair: I did that; I'll do deny it, mister. But Badger kickit me, an' Geordie, he said a bad sweir, an' made he'd cut the liver out o' me, an' catch fish wi't. It's been that way frae the first: an aith an' a bawbee was aye guid eneuch for puir Andra.

HUNT. Well, and why did they do it? I saw Jemmy dance a hornpipe on the table, and booze the company all round, when the Deacon was gone. What made you cross the fight, and play booty with your own man?

AINSLIE. Just to make him rob the Excise, mister. They're wicked, wicked men.

HUNT. And is he right for it?

AINSLIE. Ay is he.

HUNT. By jingo! When's it for?

AINSLIE. Dear, kind gentleman, I dinna rightly ken: the Deacon's that sair angered wi' me. I'm to get my orders frae Geordie the nicht.

HUNT. O, you're to get your orders from Geordie, are you? Now look here, Ainslie. You know me. I'm Hunt the Runner; I put Jemmy Rivers in the jug this morning; I've got you this evening. I mean to wind up with the Deacon. You understand? All right. Then just you listen. I'm going to take these here bracelets off, and send you home to that celebrated bed of yours. Only, as soon as you've seen the Dook you come straight round to me at Mr. Procurator-Fiscal's, and let me know the Dook's views. One word, mind, and . . . cl'k! It's a bargain?

AINSLIE. Never you fear that. I'll tak' my bannet an' come straucht to ye. Eh God, I'm glad it's nae mair nor that to start wi'. An' may the Lord bless ye, dear, kind gentleman, for your kindness. May the Lord bless ye.

HUNT. You pad the hoof.

AINSLIE (going out). An' so I wull, wulln't I not? An' bless, bless ye while there's breath in my body, wulln't I not?

HUNT (solus). You're a nice young man, Andrew Ainslie. Jemmy Rivers and the Deacon in two days! By jingo! (He dances an instant gravely, whistling to himself.) Jerry, that 'ere little two hundred of ours is as safe as the bank.

TABLEAU VI. UNMASKED

The Stage represents a room in Leslie's house. A practicable window, C., through which a band of strong moonlight falls into the room. Near the window a strong-box. A practicable door in wing, L. Candlelight.

SCENE I

LESLIE, LAWSON, MARY, seated. BRODIE at back, walking between the windows and strong-box.

LAWSON. Weel, weel, weel, weel, nae doubt.

LESLIE. Mr. Lawson, I am perfectly satisfied with Brodie's word; I will wait gladly.

LAWSON. I have nothing to say against that.

BRODIE (behind LAWSON). Nor for it.

LAWSON. For it? for it, William? Ye're perfectly richt there. (To LESLIE.) Just you do what William tells you; ye canna do better than that.

MARY. Dear uncle, I see you are vexed; but Will and I are perfectly agreed on the best course. Walter and I are young. Oh, we can wait; we can trust each other.

BRODIE (from behind). Leslie, do you think it safe to keep this strong-box in your room?

LESLIE. It does not trouble me.

BRODIE. I would not. 'Tis close to the window.

LESLIE. It's on the right side of it.

BRODIE. I give you my advice: I would not.

LAWSON. He may be right there too, Mr. Leslie.

BRODIE. I give him fair warning: it's not safe

LESLIE. I have a different treasure to concern myself about; if all goes right with that I shall be well contented.

MARY. Walter!

LAWSON. Ay, bairns, ye speak for your age.

LESLIE. Surely, sir, for every age; the ties of blood, of love, of friendship, these are life's essence.

MARY. And for no one is it truer than my uncle. If he live to be a thousand, he will still be young in heart, full of love, full of trust.

LAWSON. All, lassie, it's a wicked world.

MARY. Yes, you are out of sorts to-day; we know that.

LESLIE. Admitted that you know more of life, sir; admitted (if you please) that the world is wicked; yet you do not lose trust in those you love.

LAWSON. Weel . . . ye get gliffs, ye ken.

LESLIE. I suppose so. We can all be shaken for a time; but not, I think, in our friends. We are not deceived in them; in the few that we admit into our hearts.

MARY. Never in these.

LESLIE. We know these (to BRODIE), and we think the world of them.

BRODIE (at back). We are more acquainted with each other's tailors, believe me. You, Leslie, are a very pleasant creature. My uncle Lawson is the Procurator-Fiscal. I—What am I?—I am the Deacon of the Wrights, my ruffles are generally clean. And you think the world of me? Bravo!

LESLIE. Ay, and I think the world of you.

BRODIE (at back, pointing to LAWSON). Ask him.

LAWSON. Hoot-toot. A wheen nonsense: an honest man's an honest man, and a randy thief's a randy thief, and neither mair nor less. Mary, my lamb, it's time you were hame, and had you beauty sleep.

MARY. Do you not come with us?

LAWSON. I gang the ither gate, my lamb. (LESLIE helps MARY on with her cloak, and they say farewell at back. BRODIE for the first time comes front with LAWSON.) Sae ye've consented?

BRODIE. As you see.

LAWSON. Ye'll can pay it back?

BRODIE. I will.

LAWSON. And how? That's what I'm wonderin' to mysel'.

BRODIE. Ay, God knows that.

MARY. Come, Will.

SCENE II

LESLIE, LAWSON (wrapping up)

LESLIE. I wonder what ails Brodie?

LAWSON. How should I ken? What should I ken that ails him?

LESLIE. He seemed angry even with you.

LAWSON (impatient). Hoot awa'.

LESLIE. Of course, I know. But you see, on the very day when our engagement is announced, even the best of men may be susceptible. You yourself seem not quite pleased.

LAWSON (with great irritation). I'm perfectly pleased. I'm perfectly delighted. If I werena an auld man, I'd be just beside mysel' wi' happiness.

LESLIE. Well, I only fancied.

LAWSON. Ye had nae possible excuse to fancy. Fancy? Perfect trash and nonsense. Look at yersel'. Ye look like a ghaist, ye're white-like, ye're black aboot the een; and do ye find me deavin' ye wi' fancies? Or William Brodie either? I'll say that for him.

LESLIE. 'Tis not sorrow that alters my complexion; I've something else on hand. Come, I'll tell you, under seal. I've not been in bed till daylight for a week.

LAWSON. Weel, there's nae sense in the like o' that.

LESLIE. Gad, but there is though. Why, Procurator, this is town's business; this is a municipal affair; I'm a public character. Why? Ah, here's a nut for the Crown Prosecutor! I'm a bit of a party to a robbery.

LAWSON. Guid guide us, man, what d'ye mean?

LESLIE. You shall hear. A week ago to-night, I was passing through this very room without a candle on my way to bed, when . . . what should I see, but a masked man fumbling at that window! How he did the Lord knows. I suspect, Procurator, it was not the first he'd tried . . . for he opened it as handily as his own front door.

LAWSON. Preserve me! Another of thae robberies!

LESLIE. That's it. And, of course, I tried to seize him. But the rascal was too quick. He was down and away in an instant. You never saw a thing so daring and adroit.

LAWSON. Is that a'? Ye're a bauld lad, I'll say that for ye. I'm glad it wasna waur.

LESLIE. Yes, that's all plain sailing. But here's the hitch. Why didn't I tell the Procurator-Fiscal? You never thought of that.

LAWSON. No, man. Why?

LESLIE. Aha! There's the riddle. Will you guess? No? . . . I thought I knew the man.

LAWSON. What d'ye say?

LESLIE. I thought I knew him.

LAWSON. Wha was't?

LESLIE. Ah, there you go beyond me. That I cannot tell.

LAWSON. As God sees ye, laddie, are ye speaking truth?

LESLIE. Well . . . of course!

LAWSON. The haill truth?

LESLIE. All of it. Why not?

LAWSON. Man, I'd a kind o' gliff.

LESLIE. Why, what were you afraid of? Had you a suspicion?

LAWSON. Me? Me a suspicion? Ye're daft, sir; and me the Crown offeecial! . . . Eh man, I'm a' shakin' . . . And sae ye thocht ye kennt him?

LESLIE. I did that. And what's more, I've sat every night in case of his return. I promise you, Procurator, he shall not slip me twice. Meanwhile I'm worried and put out. You understand how such a fancy will upset a man. I'm uneasy with my friends and on bad terms with my own conscience. I keep watching, spying, comparing, putting two and two together, hunting for resemblances until my head goes round. It's like a puzzle in a dream. Only yesterday I thought I had him. And who d'you think it was?

LAWSON. Wha? Wha was't? Speak, Mr. Leslie, speak. I'm an auld man; dinna forget that.

LESLIE. I name no names. It would be unjust to him; and, upon my word, it was so silly it would be unfair to me. However, here I sit, night after night. I mean him to come back; come back he shall; and I'll tell you who he was next morning.

LAWSON. Let sleeping dogs lie, Mr. Leslie; ye dinna ken what ye micht see. And then, leave him alane, he'll come nae mair. And sitting up a' nicht . . . it's a factum imprestabile, as we say: a thing impossible to man. Gang ye to your bed, like a guid laddie, and sleep lang and soundly, and bonnie, bonnie dreams to ye! (Without.) Let sleeping dogs lie, and gang ye to your bed.

SCENE III

LESLIE

LESLIE (calling). In good time, never fear! (He carefully bolts and chains the door.) The old gentleman seems upset. What for, I wonder? Has he had a masked visitor? Why not? It's the fashion. Out with the lights. (Blows out the candles. The stage is only lighted by the moon through the window.) He is sure to come one night or other. He must come. Right or wrong, I feel it in the air. Man, but I know you, I know you somewhere. That trick of the shoulders, the hang of the clothes—whose are they? Where have I seen them? And then, that single look of the eye, that one glance about the room as the window opened . . . it is almost friendly; I have caught it over the glass's rim! If it should be . . . his? No, his it is not.

WATCHMAN (without). Past ten o'clock, and a fine moonlight night.

ANOTHER (further away). Past ten o'clock, and all's well.

LESLIE. Past ten? Ah, there's a long night before you and me, watchmen. Heavens, what a trade! But it will be something to laugh over with Mary and . . . with him? Damn it, the delusion is too strong for me. It's a thing to be ashamed of. 'We Brodies': how she says it! 'We Brodies and our Deacon': what a pride she takes in it, and how good it sounds to me! 'Deacon of his craft, sir, Deacon of the . . .! (BRODIE, masked, appears without at the window, which he proceeds to force.) Ha! I knew he'd come. I was sure of it. (He crouches near and nearer to the window, keeping in the shade.) And I know you too. I swear I know you.

SCENE IV

BRODIE, LESLIE

BRODIE enters by the window with assurance and ease, closes it silently, and proceeds to traverse the room. As he moves, LESLIE leaps upon and grapples him.

LESLIE. Take off that mask!

BRODIE. Hands off!

LESLIE. Take off the mask!

BRODIE. Leave go, by God, leave go!

LESLIE. Take it off!

BRODIE (overpowered). Leslie . . .

LESLIE. Ah! you know me! (Succeeds in tearing off the mask.) Brodie!

BRODIE (in the moonlight). Brodie.

LESLIE. You . . . you, Brodie, you?

BRODIE. Brodie, sir, Brodie as you see.

LESLIE. What does it mean? What does it mean, my God? Were you here before? Is this the second time? Are you a thief, man? are you a thief? Speak, speak, or I'll kill you.

BRODIE. I am a thief.

LESLIE. And my friend, my own friend, and . . . Mary, Mary! . . . Deacon, Deacon, for God's sake, no!

BRODIE. God help me!

LESLIE. 'We Brodies! We Brodies!'

BRODIE. Leslie—

LESLIE. Stand off! Don't touch me! You're a thief!

BRODIE. Leslie, Leslie

LESLIE. A thief's sister! Why are you here? why are you here? Tell me! Why do you not speak? Man, I know you of old. Are you Brodie, and have nothing to say?

BRODIE. To say? Not much—God help me—and commonplace, commonplace like sin. I was honest once; I made a false step; I couldn't retrace it; and . . . that is all.

LESLIE. You have forgot the bad companions!

BRODIE. I did forget them. They were there.

LESLIE. Commonplace! Commonplace! Do you speak to me, do you reason with me, do you make excuses? You—a man found out, shamed, a liar, a thief—a man that's killed me, killed this heart in my body; and you speak! What am I to do? I hold your life in my hand; have you thought of that? What am I to do?

BRODIE. Do what you please; you have me trapped.

(JEAN WATT is heard singing without two bars of 'Wanderin' Willie,' by way of signal.)

LESLIE. What is that?

BRODIE. A signal.

LESLIE. What does it mean?

BRODIE. Danger to me; there is someone coming.

LESLIE. Danger to you?

BRODIE. Some one is coming. What are you going to do with me? (A knock at the door.)

LESLIE (after a pause). Sit down. (Knocking.)

BRODIE. What are you going to do with me?

LESLIE. Sit down. (BRODIE sits in darkest part of stage. LESLIE opens door, and admits LAWSON. Door open till end of Act.)

SCENE V

BRODIE, LAWSON, LESLIE

LAWSON. This is an unco' time to come to your door; but eh, laddie, I couldna bear to think o' ye sittin' your lane in the dark.

LESLIE. It was very good of you.

LAWSON. I'm no very fond of playing hidee in the dark mysel'; and noo that I'm here—

LESLIE. I will give you a light. (He lights the candles. Lights up.)

LAWSON. God A'michty! William Brodie!

LESLIE. Yes, Brodie was good enough to watch with me.

LAWSON. But he gaed awa' . . . I dinna see . . . an' Lord be guid to us, the window's open!

LESLIE. A trap we laid for them: a device of Brodie's.

BRODIE (to LAWSON). Set a thief to catch a thief. (Passing to LESLIE, aside.) Walter Leslie, God will reward. (JEAN signals again.)

LAWSON. I dinna like that singin' at siccan a time o' the nicht.

BRODIE. I must go.

LAWSON. Not one foot o' ye. I'm ower glad to find ye in guid hands. Ay, ye dinna ken how glad.

BRODIE (aside to LESLIE). Get me out of this. There's a man there will stick at nothing.

LESLIE. Mr. Lawson, Brodie has done his shift. Why should we keep him? (JEAN appears at the door, and signs to BRODIE.)

LAWSON. Hoots! this is my trade. That's a bit o' 'Wanderin' Willie.' I've had it before me in precognitions; that same stave has been used for a signal by some o' the very warst o' them.

BRODIE (aside to LESLIE). Get me out of this. I'll never forget to-night. (JEAN at door again.)

LESLIE. Well, good-night. Brodie. When shall we meet again?

LAWSON. Not one foot o' him. (JEAN at door.) I tell you, Mr. Leslie—

SCENE VI

To these, JEAN

JEAN (from she door). Wullie, Wullie!

LAWSON. Guid guide us, Mrs. Watt! A dacent wumman like yoursel'! Whatten a time o' nicht is this to come to folks' doors?

JEAN (to BRODIE). Hawks, Wullie, hawks!

BRODIE. I suppose you know what you've done, Jean?

JEAN. I had to come, Wullie, he wadna wait another minit. He wad have come himsel'.

BRODIE. This is my mistress.

LAWSON. William, dinna tell me nae mair.

BRODIE. I have told you so much. You may as well know all. That good man knows it already. Have you issued a warrant for me . . . yet?

LAWSON. No, no, man: not another word.

BRODIE, (pointing to the window). That is my work. I am the man. Have you drawn the warrant?

LAWSON (breaking down). Your father's son!

LESLIE (to LAWSON). My good friend! Brodie, you might have spared the old man this.

BRODIE. I might have spared him years ago; and you and my sister, and myself. I might . . . would God I had! (Weeping himself.) Don't weep, my good old friend; I was lost long since; don't think of me; don't pity me; don't shame me with your pity! I began this when I was a boy. I bound the millstone round my neck; [it is irrevocable now,] and you must all suffer . . . all suffer for me! . . . [for this suffering remnant of what was once a man]. O God, that I can have fallen to stand here as I do now. My friend lying to save me from the gallows; my second father weeping tears of blood for my disgrace! And all for what? By what? Because I had an open hand, because I was a selfish dog, because I loved this woman.

JEAN. O Wullie, and she lo'ed ye weel! But come near me nae mair, come near me nae mair, my man; keep wi' your ain folks . . . your ain dacent folks.

LAWSON. Mistress Watt, ye shall sit rent free as lang's there's breath in William Lawson's body.

LESLIE. You can do one thing still . . . for Mary's sake. You can save yourself; you must fly.

BRODIE. It is my purpose; the day after to-morrow. It cannot be before. Then I will fly; and O, as God sees me, I will strive to make a new and a better life, and to be worthy of your friendship, and of your tears . . . your tears. And to be worthy of you too, Jean; for I see now that the bandage has fallen from my eyes; I see myself, O how unworthy even of you.

LESLIE. Why not to-night?

BRODIE. It cannot be before. There are many considerations. I must find money.

JEAN. Leave me, and the wean. Dinna fash yoursel' for us.

LESLIE (opening the strong-box, and pouring gold upon the table). Take this and go at once.

BRODIE. Not that . . . not the money that I came to steal!

LAWSON. Tak' it, William; I'll pay him.

BRODIE. It is in vain. I cannot leave till I have said. There is a man; I must obey him. If I slip my chain till he has done with me, the hue and cry will blaze about the country; every outport will be shut; I shall return to the gallows. He is a man that will stick at nothing.

SCENE VII

To these, MOORE

MOORE. Are you coming?

BRODIE. I am coming.

MOORE (appearing in the door). Do you want us all to get thundering well scragged?

BRODIE (going). There is my master.

ACT - CURTAIN DROP.

ACT IV.

TABLEAU VII. THE ROBBERY

The Stage represents the outside of the Excise Office in Chessel's Court. At the back, L.C., an archway opening on the High Street. The door of the Excise in wing, R.; the opposite side of the stage is lumbered with barrels, packing-cases, etc. Moonlight; the Excise Office casts a shadow over half the stage. A clock strikes the hour. A round of the City Guard, with halberts, lanterns, etc., enters and goes out again by the arch, after having examined the fastenings of the great door and the lumber on the left. Cry without in the High Street: 'Ten by the bell, and a fine clear night.' Then enter cautiously by the arch, SMITH and MOORE, with AINSLIE loaded with tools.

SCENE I

SMITH, MOORE, AINSLIE

SMITH (entering first). Come on. Coast clear.

MOORE (after they have come to the front.) Ain't he turned up yet?

SMITH (to AINSLIE). Now Maggot! The fishing's a going to begin.

AINSLIE. Dinna cangle, Geordie. My back's fair broke.

MOORE. O muck! Hand out them pieces.

SMITH. All right, Humptious! (To AINSLIE.) You're a nice old sort for a rag-and-bone man: can't hold a bag open! (Taking out tools.) Here they was. Here are the bunchums, one and two; and jolly old keys was they. Here's the picklocks, crow-bars, and here's Lord George's pet bull's eye, his old and valued friend, the Cracksman's treasure!

MOORE. Just like you. Forgot the rotten centrebit.

SMITH. That's all you know. Here she is, bless her! Portrait of George as a gay hironmonger.

MOORE. O rot! Hand it over, and keep yourself out of that there thundering moonlight.

SMITH (lighting lantern). All right, old mumble-peg. Don't you get carried away by the fire of old Rome. That's your motto. Here are the tools; a perfect picter of the sublime and beautiful; and all I hope is, that our friend and pitcher, the Deakin, will make a better job of it than he did last night. If he don't, I shall retire from the business—that's all; and it'll be George and his little wife and a black footman till death do us part.

MOORE. O muck! You're all jaw like a sheep's jimmy. That's my opinion of you. When did you see him last?

SMITH. This morning; and he looked as if he was rehearsing for his own epitaph. I never see such a change in a man. I gave him the office for to-night; and was he grateful? Did he weep upon my faithful bosom? No; he smiled upon me like a portrait of the dear departed. I see his 'art was far away; and it broke my own to look at him.

MOORE. Muck! Wot I ses is, if a cove's got that much of the nob about him, wot's the good of his working single-handed? That's wot's the matter with him.

SMITH. Well, old Father Christmas, he ain't single-handed to-night, is he?

MOORE. No, he ain't; he's got a man with him to-night.

SMITH. Pardon me, Romeo; two men, I think?

MOORE. A man wot means business. If I'd a bin with him last night, it ain't psalm-singin' would have got us off. Psalm-singin'? Muck! Let 'em try it on with me.

AINSLIE. Losh me, I heard a noise. (Alarm; they crouch into the shadow and listen.)

SMITH. All serene. (To AINSLIE) Am I to cut that liver out of you? Now, am I? (A whistle.) 'St! here we are. (Whistles a modulation, which is answered.)

SCENE II

To these BRODIE

MOORE. Waiting for you, Deacon.

BRODIE. I see. Everything ready?

SMITH. All a-growing and a-blowing.

BRODIE. Give me the light. (Briefly examines tools and door with bull's eye.) You, George, stand by, and hand up the pieces. Ainslie, take the glim. Moore, out and watch.

MOORE. I didn't come here to do sentry-go, I didn't.

BRODIE. You came here to do as I tell you. (MOORE goes up slowly.) Second bunch, George. I know the lock. Steady with the glim. (At work.) No good. Give me the centrebit.

SMITH. Right. (Work continues. AINSLIE drops lantern.)

BRODIE. Curse you! (Throttling and kicking him.) You shake, and you shake, and you can't even hold a light for your betters. Hey?

AINSLIE. Eh Deacon, Deacon . . .

SMITH. Now Ghost! (With lantern.)

BRODIE. 'St, Moore!

MOORE. Wot's the row?

BRODIE. Take you the light.

MOORE (to AINSLIE). Wo' j' yer shakin' at? (Kicks him.)

BRODIE (to AINSLIE). Go you, and see if you're good at keeping watch. Inside the arch. And if you let a footfall pass, I'll break your back. (AINSLIE retires.) Steady with the light. (At work with centrebit.) Hand up number four, George. (At work with picklock.) That has it.

SMITH. Well done our side.

BRODIE. Now the crow bar! (At work.) That's it. Put down the glim, Badger, and help at the wrench. Your whole weight, men! Put your backs to it! (While they work at the bar, BRODIE stands by, dusting his hands with a pocket-handkerchief. As the door opens.) Voilà! In with you.

MOORE (entering with light). Mucking fine work too, Deacon!

BRODIE. Take up the irons, George!

SMITH. How about the P(h)antom?

BRODIE. Leave him to me. I'll give him a look. (Enters office.)

SMITH (following). Houp-là!

SCENE III

AINSLIE; afterwards BRODIE; afterwards HUNT and OFFICERS

AINSLIE. Ca' ye that mainners? Ye're grand gentry by your way o't! Eh sirs, my hench! Ay, that was the Badger. Man, but ye'll look bonnie hangin'! (A faint whistle.) Lord's sake, what's thon? Ay, it'll be Hunt an' his lads. (Whistle repeated.) Losh me, what gars him whustle, whustle? Does he think me deaf? (Goes up. BRODIE enters from office, stands an instant, and sees him making a signal through the arch.)

BRODIE. Rats! Rats! (Hides L. among lumber. Enter noiselessly through arch HUNT and OFFICERS.)

HUNT. Birds caught?

AINSLIE. They're a' ben the house, mister.

HUNT. All three?

AINSLIE. The hale set, mister.

BRODIE. Liar!

HUNT. Mum, lads, and follow me. (Exit, with his men, into office. BRODIE seen with dagger.)

HUNT (within). In the King's name!

MOORE (within). Muck!

SMITH (within). Go it, Badger.

HUNT (within). Take 'em alive, boys!

AINSLIE. Eh, but that's awful. (The Deacon leaps out, and stabs him. He falls without a cry.)

BRODIE. Saved! (He goes out by the arch.)

SCENE IV

HUNT and OFFICERS, with SMITH and MOORE handcuffed. Signs of a severe struggle

HUNT (entering). Bring 'em along, lads! (Looking at prisoners with lantern.) Pleased to see you again, Badger. And you too, George. But I'd rather have seen your principal. Where's he got to?

MOORE. To hell, I hope.

HUNT. Always the same pretty flow of language, I see, Hump. (Looking at burglary with lantern.) A very tidy piece of work, Dook; very tidy! Much too good for you. Smacks of a fine tradesman. It was the Deacon, I suppose?

SMITH. You ought to know G. S. better by this time, Jerry.

HUNT. All right, your Grace: we'll talk it over with the Deacon himself. Where's the jackal? Here, you, Ainslie! Where are you? By jingo, I thought as much. Stabbed to the heart and dead as a herring!

SMITH. Bravo!

HUNT. More of the Deacon's work, I guess? Does him credit too, don't it, Badger?

MOORE. Muck. Was that the thundering cove that peached?

HUNT. That was the thundering cove.

MOORE. And is he corpsed?

HUNT. I should just about reckon he was.

MOORE. Then, damme, I don't mind swinging!

HUNT. We'll talk about that presently. M'Intyre and Stewart, you get a stretcher, and take that rubbish to the office. Pick it up; it's only a dead informer. Hand these two gentlemen over to Mr. Procurator-Fiscal, with Mr. Jerry Hunt's compliments. Johnstone and Syme, you come along with me. I'll bring the Deacon round myself.

ACT - CURTAIN DROP.

ACT V.

TABLEAU VIII. THE OPEN DOOR

The Stage represents the Deacon's room, as in Tableau I. Fire light. Stage dark. A pause. Then knocking at the door, C. Cries without of 'WILLIE!' 'MR. BRODIE!' The door is burst open.

SCENE I

DOCTOR, MARY, a MAIDSERVANT with lights.

DOCTOR. The apartment is unoccupied.

MARY. Dead, and he not here!

DOCTOR. The bed has not been slept in. The counterpane is not turned down.

MARY. It is not true; it cannot be true.

DOCTOR. My dear young lady, you must have misunderstood your brother's language.

MARY. O no; that I did not. That I am sure I did not.

DOCTOR (looking at door). The strange thing is . . . the bolt.

SERVANT. It's unco strange.

DOCTOR. Well, we have acted for the best.

SERVANT. Sir, I dinna think this should gang nae further.

DOCTOR. The secret is in our keeping. Affliction is enough without scandal.

MARY. Kind heaven, what does it mean?

DOCTOR. I think there is no more to be done.

MARY. I am here alone, Doctor; you pass my uncle's door?

DOCTOR. The Procurator-Fiscal? I shall make it my devoir. Expect him soon. (Goes out with MAID.)

MARY (hastily searches the room). No, he is not there. She was right! O father, you can never know, praise God!

SCENE II

MARY, to whom JEAN and afterwards LESLIE

JEAN (at door). Mistress . . . !

MARY. Ah! Who is there? Who are you?

JEAN. Is he no hame yet? I'm aye waitin' on him.

MARY. Waiting for him? Do you know the Deacon? You?

JEAN. I maun see him. Eh, lassie, it's life and death.

MARY. Death . . . O my heart!

JEAN. I maun see him, bonnie leddie. I'm a puir body, and no fit to be seen speakin' wi' the likes o' you. But O lass, ye are the Deacon's sister, and ye hae the Deacon's e'en, and for the love of the dear kind Lord, let's in and hae a word wi' him ere it be ower late. I'm bringin' siller.

MARY. Siller? You? For him? O father, father, if you could hear! What are you? What are you . . . to him?

JEAN. I'll be the best frien' 'at ever he had; for, O dear leddie, I wad gie my bluid to help him.

MARY. And the . . . the child?

JEAN. The bairn?

MARY. Nothing! O nothing! I am in trouble, and I know not what I say. And I cannot help you; I cannot help you if I would. He is not here; and I believed he was; and ill . . . ill; and he is not—he is . . . O, I think I shall lose my mind!

JEAN. Ay, it's unco business.

MARY. His father is dead within there . . . dead, I tell you . . . dead!

JEAN. It's mebbe just as weel.

MARY. Well? Well? Has it come to this? O Walter, Walter! come back to me, or I shall die. (LESLIE enters, C.)

LESLIE. Mary, Mary! I hoped to have spared you this. (To JEAN.) What—you? Is he not here?

JEAN. I'm aye waitin' on him.

LESLIE. What has become of him? Is he mad? Where is he?

JEAN. The Lord A'michty kens, Mr. Leslie. But I maun find him; I maun find him.

SCENE III

MARY, LESLIE

MARY. O Walter, Walter! What does it mean?

LESLIE. You have been a brave girl all your life, Mary; you must lean on me . . . you must trust in me . . . and be a brave girl till the end.

MARY. Who is she? What does she want with him? And he . . . where is he? Do you know that my father is dead, and the Deacon not here? Where has he gone? He may be dead, too. Father, brother . . . O God, it is more than I can bear!

LESLIE. Mary, my dear, dear girl . . . when will you be my wife?

MARY. O, do not speak . . . not speak . . . of it to-night. Not to-night! O not to-night!

LESLIE. I know, I know dear heart! And do you think that I whom you have chosen, I whose whole life is in your love—do you think that I would press you now if there were not good cause?

MARY. Good cause! Something has happened. Something has happened . . . to him! Walter . . . ! Is he . . . dead?

LESLIE. There are worse things in the world than death. There is O . . . Mary, he is your brother!

MARY. What? Dishonour! . . . The Deacon! . . . My God!

LESLIE. My wife, my wife!

MARY. No, no! Keep away from me. Don't touch me. I'm not fit . . . not fit to be near you. What has he done? I am his sister. Tell me the worst. Tell me the worst at once.

LESLIE. That, if God wills, dear, that you shall never know. Whatever it be, think that I knew it all, and only loved you better; think that your true husband is with you, and you are not to bear it alone.

MARY. My husband? . . . Never.

LESLIE. Mary . . . !

MARY. You forget, you forget what I am. I am his sister. I owe him a lifetime of happiness and love; I owe him even you. And whatever his fault, however ruinous his disgrace, he is my brother—my own brother—and my place is still with him.

LESLIE. Your place is with me—is with your husband. With me, with me; and for his sake most of all. What can you do for him alone? how can you help him alone? It wrings my heart to think how little. But together is different. Together . . . I join my strength, my will, my courage to your own, and together we may save him.

MARY. All that is over. Once I was blessed among women. I was my father's daughter, my brother loved me, I lived to be your wife. Now . . . ! My father is dead, my brother is shamed; and you . . . O how could I face the world, how could I endure myself, if I preferred my happiness to your honour?

LESLIE. What is my honour but your happiness? In what else does it consist? Is it in denying me my heart? is it in visiting another's sin upon the innocent? Could I do that, and be my mother's son? Could I do that, and bear my father's name? Could I do that, and have ever been found worthy of you?

MARY. It is my duty . . . my duty. Why will you make it so hard for me? So hard, Walter so hard!

LESLIE. Do I pursue you only for your good fortune, your beauty, the credit of your friends, your family's good name? That were not love, and I love you. I love you, dearest, I love you. Friend, father, brother, husband . . . I must be all these to you. I am a man who can love well.

MARY. Silence . . . in pity! I cannot . . . O, I cannot bear it.

LESLIE. And say it was I who had fallen. Say I had played my neck and lost it . . . that I were pushed by the law to the last limits of ignominy and despair. Whose love would sanctify my jail to me? whose pity would shine upon me in the dock? whose prayers would accompany me to the gallows? Whose but yours? Yours! . . . And you would entreat me—me!—to do what you shrink from even in thought, what you would die ere you attempted in deed!

MARY. Walter . . . on my knees . . . no more, no more!

LESLIE. My wife! my wife! Here on my heart! It is I that must kneel . . . I that must kneel to you.

MARY. Dearest! . . . Husband! You forgive him? O, you forgive him?

LESLIE. He is my brother now. Let me take you to our father. Come.

SCENE IV

After a pause, BRODIE, through the window

BRODIE. Saved! And the alibi! Man, but you've been near it this time—near the rope, near the rope. Ah boy, it was your neck, your neck you fought for. They were closing hell-doors upon me, swift as the wind, when I slipped through and shot for heaven! Saved! The dog that sold me, I settled him; and the other dogs are staunch. Man, but your alibi will stand! Is the window fast? The neighbours must not see the Deacon, the poor, sick Deacon, up and stirring at this time o' night. Ay, the good old room in the good, cozy old house . . . and the rat a dead rat, and all saved. (He lights the candles.) Your hand shakes, sir? Fie! And you saved, and you snug and sick in your bed, and it but a dead rat after all? (He takes off his hanger and lays it on the table.) Ay, it was a near touch. Will it come to the dock? If it does! You've a tongue, and you've a head, and you've an alibi; and your alibi will stand. (He takes off his coat, takes out the dagger, and with a gesture of striking) Home! He fell without a sob. 'He breaketh them against the bosses of his buckler!' (Lays the dagger on the table.) Your alibi . . . ah Deacon, that's your life! . . . your alibi, your alibi. (He takes up a candle and turns towards the door.) O! . . . Open, open, open! judgment of God, the door is open!

SCENE V

BRODIE, MARY.

BRODIE. Did you open the door?

MARY. I did.

BRODIE. You . . . you opened the door?

MARY. I did open it

BRODIE. Were you . . . alone?

MARY. I was not. The servant was with me; and the doctor.

BRODIE. O . . . the servant . . . and the doctor. Very true. Then it's all over the town by now. The servant and the doctor. The doctor? What doctor? Why the doctor?

MARY. My father is dead. O Will, where have you been?

BRODIE. Your father is dead. O yes! He's dead, is he? Dead. Quite right. Quite right . . . How did you open the door? It's strange. I bolted it.

MARY. We could not help it, Will, now could we? The doctor forced it. He had to, had he not?

BRODIE. The doctor forced it? The doctor? Was he here? He forced it? He?

MARY. We did it for the best; it was I who did it . . . I, your own sister. And O Will, my Willie, where have you been? You have not been in any harm, any danger?

BRODIE. Danger? O my young lady, you have taken care of that. It's not danger now, it's death. Death? Ah! Death! Death! Death! (Clutching the table. Then, recovering as from a dream.) Death? Did you say my father was dead? My father? O my God, my poor old father! Is he dead, Mary? Have I lost him? is he gone? O, Mary dear, and to think of where his son was!

MARY. Dearest, he is in heaven.

BRODIE. Did he suffer?

MARY. He died like a child. Your name . . . it was his last.

BRODIE. My name? Mine? O Mary, if he had known! He knows now. He knows; he sees us now . . . sees me! Ay, and sees you, left how lonely!

MARY. Not so, dear; not while you live. Wherever you are, I shall not be alone, so you live.

BRODIE. While I live? I? The old house is ruined, and the old master dead, and I! . . . O Mary, try and believe I did not mean that it should come to this; try and believe that I was only weak at first. At first? And now! The good old man dead, the kind sister ruined, the innocent boy fallen, fallen . . . ! You will be quite alone; all your old friends, all the old faces, gone into darkness. The night (with a gesture) . . . it waits for me. You will be quite alone.

MARY. The night!

BRODIE. Mary, you must hear. How am I to tell her, and the old man just dead! Mary, I was the boy you knew; I loved pleasure, I was weak; I have fallen . . . low . . . lower than you think. A beginning is so small a thing! I never dreamed it would come to this . . . this hideous last night.

MARY. Willie, you must tell me, dear. I must have the truth . . . the kind truth . . . at once . . . in pity.

BRODIE. Crime. I have fallen. Crime.

MARY. Crime?

BRODIE. Don't shrink from me. Miserable dog that I am, selfish hound that has dragged you to this misery . . . you and all that loved him . . . think only of my torments, think only of my penitence, don't shrink from me.

MARY. I do not care to hear, I do not wish, I do not mind; you are my brother. What do I care? How can I help you?

BRODIE. Help? help me? You would not speak of it, not wish it, if you knew. My kind good sister, my little playmate, my sweet friend! was I ever unkind to you till yesterday? Not openly unkind? you'll say that when I am gone.

MARY. If you have done wrong, what do I care? If you have failed, does it change my twenty years of love and worship? Never!

BRODIE. Yet I must make her understand . . . !

MARY. I am your true sister, dear. I cannot fail, I will never leave you, I will never blame you. Come! (Goes to embrace.)

BRODIE (recoiling). No, don't touch me, not a finger, not that, anything but that!

MARY. Willie, Willie!

BRODIE (taking the bloody dagger from the table). See, do you understand that?

MARY. Ah! What, what is it!

BRODIE. Blood. I have killed a man.

MARY. You? . . .

BRODIE. I am a murderer; I was a thief before. Your brother . . . the old man's only son!

MARY. Walter, Walter, come to me!

BRODIE. Now you see that I must die; now you see that I stand upon the grave's edge, all my lost life behind me, like a horror to think upon, like a frenzy, like a dream that is past. And you, you are alone. Father, brother, they are gone from you; one to heaven, one . . . !

MARY. Hush, dear, hush! Kneel, pray; it is not too late to repent. Think of our father dear; repent. (She weeps, straining to his bosom.) O Willie, my darling boy, repent and join us.

SCENE VI

To these, LAWSON, LESLIE, JEAN

LAWSON. She kens a', thank the guid Lord!

BRODIE (to MARY). I know you forgive me now; I ask no more. That is a good man. (To LESLIE.) Will you take her from my hands? (LESLIE takes MARY.) Jean, are ye here to see the end?

JEAN. Eh man, can ye no fly? Could ye no say that it was me?

BRODIE. No, Jean, this is where it ends. Uncle, this is where it ends. And to think that not an hour ago I still had hopes! Hopes! Ay, not an hour ago I thought of a new life. You were not forgotten, Jean. Leslie, you must try to forgive me . . . you, too!

LESLIE. You are her brother.

BRODIE (to LAWSON). And you?

LAWSON. My name-child and my sister's bairn!

BRODIE. You won't forget Jean, will you? nor the child?

LAWSON. That I will not.

MARY. O Willie, nor I.

SCENE VII

To these, HUNT

HUNT. The game's up, Deacon. I'll trouble you to come along with me.

BRODIE (behind the table). One moment, officer: I have a word to say before witnesses ere I go. In all this there is but one man guilty; and that man is I. None else has sinned; none else must suffer. This poor woman (pointing to JEAN) I have used; she never understood. Mr. Procurator-Fiscal, that is my dying confession. (He snatches his hanger from the table, and rushes upon HUNT, who parries, and runs him through. He reels across the stage and falls.) The new life . . . the new life! (He dies.)

CURTAIN.

BEAU AUSTIN

DEDICATED WITH ADMIRATION AND RESPECT TO GEORGE MEREDITH

BOURNEMOUTH: 1st October 1884.

PERSONS REPRESENTED
GEORGE FREDERICK AUSTIN, called 'Beau Austin'
JOHN FENWICK, of Allonby Shaw
ANTHONY MUSGRAVE, Cornet in the Prince's Own
MENTEITH, the Beau's Valet

A ROYAL DUKE (Dumb show.)
DOROTHY MUSGRAVE, Anthony's Sister
MISS EVELINA FOSTER, her Aunt
BARBARA RIDLEY, her Maid
VISITORS TO THE WELLS

The Time is 1820. The Scene is laid at Tunbridge Wells. The Action occupies a space of ten hours.

HAYMARKET THEATRE

Monday, November 3d, 1890

CAST

GEORGE FREDERICK AUSTIN	Mr. TREE
JOHN FENWICK	Mr. FRED TERRY
ANTHONY MUSGRAVE	Mr. EDMUND MAURICE
MENTEITH	Mr. BROOKFIELD
A ROYAL DUKE	Mr. ROBB HARWOOD
DOROTHY MUSGRAVE	Mrs. TREE
MISS EVELINA FOSTER	Miss ROSE LECLERCQ
BARBARA RIDLEY	Miss AYLWARD
VISITORS TO THE WELLS	

PROLOGUE

Spoken by MR. TREE in the character of Beau Austin

'To all and singular,' as Dryden says,
We bring a fancy of those Georgian days,
Whose style still breathed a faint and fine perfume
Of old-world courtliness and old-world bloom:
When speech was elegant and talk was fit
For slang had not been canonised as wit;
When manners reigned, when breeding had the wall,
And Women—yes!—were ladies first of all;
When Grace was conscious of its gracefulness,
And man—though Man!—was not ashamed to dress.
A brave formality, a measured ease,
Were his—and her's—whose effort was to please.
And to excel in pleasing was to reign
And, if you sighed, never to sigh in vain.

But then, as now—it may be, something more—
Woman and man were human to the core.
The hearts that throbbed behind that quaint attire
Burned with a plenitude of essential fire.
They too could risk, they also could rebel,

They could love wisely—they could love too well.
In that great duel of Sex, that ancient strife
Which is the very central fact of life,
They could—and did—engage it breath for breath,
They could—and did—get wounded unto death.
As at all times since time for us began
Woman was truly woman, man was man,
And joy and sorrow were as much at home
In trifling Tunbridge as in mighty Rome.

Dead—dead and done with!
Swift from shine to shade
The roaring generations flit and fade.
To this one, fading, flitting, like the rest,
We come to proffer—be it worst or best—
A sketch, a shadow, of one brave old time;
A hint of what it might have held sublime;
A dream, an idyll, call it what you will,
Of man still Man, and woman—Woman still!

ACT I.

MUSICAL INDUCTION: 'Lascia ch'io pianga' (Rinaldo).

HANDEL.

The Stage represents Miss Foster's apartments at the Wells. Doors, L. and C.; a window, L. C., looking on the street; a table R., laid for breakfast.

SCENE I

BARBARA; to her MISS FOSTER

BARBARA (out of window). Mr. Menteith! Mr. Menteith! Mr. Menteith!—Drat his old head! Will nothing make him hear?—Mr. Menteith!

MISS FOSTER (entering). Barbara! this is incredible: after all my lessons, to be leaning from the window, and calling (for unless my ears deceived me, you were positively calling!) into the street.

BARBARA. Well, madam, just wait until you hear who it was. I declare it was much more for Miss Dorothy and yourself than for me; and if it was a little countrified, I had a good excuse.

MISS FOSTER. Nonsense, child! At least, who was it?

BARBARA. Miss Evelina, I was sure you would ask. Well, what do you think? I was looking out of window at the barber's opposite—

MISS FOSTER. Of which I entirely disapprove—

BARBARA. And first there came out two of the most beautiful—the Royal livery, madam!

MISS FOSTER. Of course, of course: the Duke of York arrived last night. I trust you did not hail the Duke's footmen?

BARBARA. O no, madam, it was after they were gone. Then, who should come out—but you'll never guess!

MISS FOSTER. I shall certainly not try.

BARBARA. Mr. Menteith himself!

MISS FOSTER. Why, child, I never heard of him.

BARBARA. O madam, not the Beau's own gentleman?

MISS FOSTER. Mr. Austin's servant. No? Is it possible? By that, George Austin must be here.

BARBARA. No doubt of that, madam; they're never far apart. He came out feeling his chin, madam, so; and a packet of letters under his arm, so; and he had the Beau's own walk to that degree you couldn't tell his back from his master's.

MISS FOSTER. My dear Barbara, you too frequently forget yourself. A young woman in your position must beware of levity.

BARBARA. Madam, I know it; but la, what are you to make of me? Look at the time and trouble dear Miss Dorothy was always taking—she that trained up everybody—and see what's come of it: Barbara Ridley I was, and Barbara Ridley I am; and I don't do with fashionable ways—I can't do with them; and indeed, Miss Evelina, I do sometimes wish we were all back again on Edenside, and Mr. Anthony a boy again, and dear Miss Dorothy her old self, galloping the bay mare along the moor, and taking care of all of us as if she was our mother, bless her heart!

MISS FOSTER. Miss Dorothy herself, child? Well, now you mention it, Tunbridge of late has scarcely seemed to suit her constitution. She falls away, has not a word to throw at a dog, and is ridiculously pale. Well, now Mr. Austin has returned, after six months of infidelity to the dear Wells, we shall all, I hope, be brightened up. Has the mail come?

BARBARA. That it has, madam, and the sight of Mr. Menteith put it clean out of my head. (With letters.) Four for you, Miss Evelina, two for me, and only one for Miss Dorothy. Miss Dorothy seems quite neglected, does she not? Six months ago, it was a different story.

MISS FOSTER. Well, and that's true, Barbara, and I had not remarked it. I must take her seriously to task. No young lady in her position should neglect her correspondence. (Opening a letter.) Here's from that dear ridiculous boy, the Cornet, announcing his arrival for to-day.

BARBARA. O madam, will he come in his red coat?

MISS FOSTER. I could not conceive him missing such a chance. Youth, child, is always vain, and Mr. Anthony is unusually young.

BARBARA. La, madam, he can't help that.

MISS FOSTER. My child, I am not so sure. Mr. Anthony is a great concern to me. He was orphaned, to be sure, at ten years old; and ever since he has been only as it were his sister's son. Dorothy did everything for him: more indeed than I thought quite ladylike, but I suppose I begin to be old-fashioned. See how she worked and slaved—yes, slaved!—for him: teaching him herself, with what pains and patience she only could reveal, and learning that she might be able; and see what he is now: a gentleman, of course, but, to be frank, a very commonplace one: not what I had hoped of Dorothy's brother; not what I had dreamed of the heir of two families—Musgrave and Foster, child! Well, he may now meet Mr. Austin. He requires a Mr. Austin to embellish and correct his manners. (Opening another letter.) Why, Barbara, Mr. John Scrope and Miss Kate Dacre are to be married!

BARBARA. La, madam, how nice!

MISS FOSTER. They are: As I'm a sinful woman. And when will you be married, Barbara? and when dear Dorothy? I hate to see old maids a-making.

BARBARA. La, Miss Evelina, there's no harm in an old maid.

MISS FOSTER. You speak like a fool, child: sour grapes are all very well but it's a woman's business to be married. As for Dorothy, she is five-and-twenty, and she breaks my heart. Such a match, too! Ten thousand to her fortune, the best blood in the north, a most advantageous person, all the graces, the finest sensibility, excellent judgment, the Foster walk; and all these to go positively a-begging! The men seem stricken with blindness. Why, child, when I came out (and I was the dear girl's image!) I had more swains at my feet in a fortnight than our Dorothy in—O, I cannot fathom it: it must be the girl's own fault.

BARBARA. Why, madam, I did think it was a case with Mr. Austin.

MISS FOSTER. With Mr. Austin? why, how very rustic! The attentions of a gentleman like Mr. Austin, child, are not supposed to lead to matrimony. He is a feature of society: an ornament: a personage: a private gentleman by birth, but a kind of king by habit and reputation. What woman could he marry? Those to whom he might properly aspire are all too far below him. I have known George Austin too long, child, and I understand that the very greatness of his success condemns him to remain unmarried.

BARBARA. Sure, madam, that must be tiresome for him.

MISS FOSTER. Some day, child, you will know better than to think so. George Austin, as I conceive him, and as he is regarded by the world, is one of the triumphs of the other sex. I walked my first minuet with him: I wouldn't tell you the year, child, for worlds; but it was soon after his famous rencounter with Colonel Villiers. He had killed his man, he wore pink and silver, was most elegantly pale, and the most ravishing creature!

BARBARA. Well, madam, I believe that: he is the most beautiful gentleman still.

SCENE II

To these, DOROTHY, L

DOROTHY (entering) Good-morning, aunt! Is there anything for me? (She goes eagerly to table, and looks at letters.)

MISS FOSTER. Good-morrow, niece. Breakfast, Barbara.

DOROTHY (with letter unopened). Nothing.

MISS FOSTER. And what do you call that, my dear? (Sitting.) Is John Fenwick nobody?

DOROTHY (looking at letter.) From John? O yes, so it is. (Lays down letter unopened, and sits to breakfast, BARBARA waiting.)

MISS FOSTER (to BARBARA, with plate). Thanks, child; now you may give me some tea. Dolly, I must insist on your eating a good breakfast: I cannot away with your pale cheeks and that Patience-on-a Monument kind of look. (Toast, Barbara.) At Edenside you ate and drank and looked like Hebe. What have you done with your appetite?

DOROTHY. I don't know, aunt, I'm sure.

MISS FOSTER. Then consider, please, and recover it as soon as you can: to a young lady in your position a good appetite is an attraction—almost a virtue. Do you know that your brother arrives this morning?

DOROTHY. Dear Anthony! Where is his letter, Aunt Evelina? I am pleased that he should leave London and its perils, if only for a day.

MISS FOSTER. My dear, there are moments when you positively amaze. (Barbara, some pâté, if you please!) I beg you not to be a prude. All women, of course, are virtuous; but a prude is something I regard with abhorrence. The Cornet is seeing life, which is exactly what he wanted. You brought him up surprisingly well; I have always admired you for it; but let us admit—as women of the world, my dear—it was no upbringing for a man. You and that fine solemn fellow, John Fenwick, led a life that was positively no better than the Middle Ages; and between the two of you, poor Anthony (who, I am sure, was a most passive creature!) was so packed with principle and admonition that I vow and declare he reminded me of Issachar stooping between his two burdens. It was high time for him to be done with your apron-string, my dear: he has all his wild oats to sow; and that is an occupation which it is unwise to defer too long. By the bye, have you heard the news? The Duke of York has done us a service for which I was unprepared. (More tea, Barbara!) George Austin, bringing the prince in his train, is with us once more.

DOROTHY. I knew he was coming.

MISS FOSTER. You knew, child? and did not tell? You are a public criminal.

DOROTHY. I did not think it mattered, Aunt Evelina.

MISS FOSTER. O do not make-believe. I am in love with him myself, and have been any time since Nelson and the Nile. As for you, Dolly, since he went away six months ago, you have been positively in the megrims. I shall date your loss of appetite from George Austin's vanishing. No, my dear, our family require entertainment: we must have wit about us, and beauty, and the bel air.

BARBARA. Well, Miss Dorothy, perhaps it's out of my place: but I do hope Mr. Austin will come: I should love to have him see my necklace on.

DOROTHY. Necklace? what necklace? Did he give you a necklace?

BARBARA. Yes, indeed, Miss, that he did: the very same day that he drove you in his curricle to Penshurst. You remember, Miss, I couldn't go.

DOROTHY. I remember.

MISS FOSTER. And so do I. I had a touch of . . . Foster in the blood: the family gout, dears! . . . And you, you ungrateful nymph, had him a whole day to yourself, and not a word to tell me when you returned.

DOROTHY. I remember. (Rising.) Is that the necklace, Barbara? It does not suit you. Give it me.

BARBARA. La, Miss Dorothy, I wouldn't for the world.

DOROTHY. Come, give it me. I want it. Thank you: you shall have my birthday pearls instead.

MISS FOSTER. Why, Dolly, I believe you're jealous of the maid. Foster, Foster: always a Foster trick to wear the willow in anger.

DOROTHY. I do not think, madam, that I am of a jealous habit.

MISS FOSTER. O, the personage is your excuse! And I can tell you, child, that when George Austin was playing Florizel to the Duchess's Perdita, all the maids in England fell a prey to green-eyed melancholy. It was the ton, you see: not to pine for that Sylvander was to resign from good society.

DOROTHY. Aunt Evelina, stop; I cannot endure to hear you. What is he after all but just Beau Austin? What has he done—with half a century of good health, what has he done that is either memorable or worthy? Diced and danced and set fashions; vanquished in a drawing-room, fought for a word; what else? As if these were the meaning of life! Do not make me think so poorly of all of us women. Sure, we can rise to admire a better kind of man than Mr. Austin. We are not all to be snared with the eye, dear aunt; and those that are—O! I know not whether I more hate or pity them.

MISS FOSTER. You will give me leave, my niece: such talk is neither becoming in a young lady nor creditable to your understanding. The world was made a great while before Miss Dorothy Musgrave; and you will do much better to ripen your opinions, and in the meantime read your letter, which I perceive you have not opened. (DOROTHY opens and reads letter.) Barbara, child, you should not listen at table.

BARBARA. Sure, madam, I hope I know my place.

MISS FOSTER. Then do not do it again.

DOROTHY. Poor John Fenwick! he coming here!

MISS FOSTER. Well, and why not? Dorothy, my darling child, you give me pain. You never had but one chance, let me tell you pointedly: and that was John Fenwick. If I were you, I would not let my vanity so blind me. This is not the way to marry.

DOROTHY. Dear aunt, I shall never marry.

MISS FOSTER. A fiddlestick's end! every one must marry. (Rising.) Are you for the Pantiles?

DOROTHY. Not to-day, dear,

MISS FOSTER. Well, well! have your wish, Dolorosa. Barbara, attend and dress me.

SCENE III

DOROTHY

DOROTHY. How she tortures me, poor aunt, my poor blind aunt; and I—I could break her heart with a word. That she should see nothing, know nothing—there's where it kills. O, it is more than I can bear . . . and yet, how much less than I deserve! Mad girl, of what do I complain? that this dear innocent woman still believes me good, still pierces me to the soul with trustfulness. Alas, and were it otherwise, were her dear eyes opened to the truth, what were left me but death?—He, too—she must still be praising him, and every word is a lash upon my conscience. If I could die of my secret: if I could cease—but one moment cease—this living lie; if I could sleep and forget and be at rest!— Poor John! (reading the letter) he at least is guiltless; and yet for my fault he too must suffer, he too must bear part in my shame. Poor John Fenwick! Has he come back with the old story: with what might have been, perhaps, had we stayed by Edenside? Eden? yes, my Eden, from which I fell. O my old north country, my old river—the river of my innocence, the old country of my hopes—how could I endure to look on you now? And how to meet John?—John, with the old love on his lips, the old, honest, innocent, faithful heart! There was a Dorothy once who was not unfit to ride with him, her heart as light as his, her life as clear as the bright rivers we forded; he called her his Diana, he crowned her so with rowan. Where is that Dorothy now? that Diana? she that was everything to John? For O, I did him good; I know I did him good; I will still believe I did him good: I made him honest and kind and a true man; alas, and could not guide myself! And now, how will he despise me! For he shall know; if I die, he shall know all; I could not live, and not be true with him. (She takes out the necklace and looks at it.) That he should have bought me from my maid! George, George, that you should have stooped to this! Basely as you have used me, this is the basest. Perish the witness! (She treads the trinket under foot.) Break, break like my heart, break like my hopes, perish like my good name!

SCENE IV

To her, FENWICK, C.

FENWICK (after a pause). Is this how you receive me, Dorothy? Am I not welcome?—Shall I go then?

DOROTHY (running to him, with hands outstretched). O no, John, not for me. (Turning, and pointing to the necklace.) But you find me changed.

FENWICK (with a movement towards the necklace). This?

DOROTHY. No, no, let it lie. That is a trinket—broken. But the old Dorothy is dead.

FENWICK. Dead, dear? Not to me.

DOROTHY. Dead to you—dead to all men.

FENWICK. Dorothy, I loved you as a boy. There is not a meadow on Edenside but is dear to me for your sake, not a cottage but recalls your goodness, not a rock nor a tree but brings back something of the best and brightest youth man ever had. You were my teacher and my queen; I walked with you, I talked with you, I rode with you; I lived in your shadow; I saw with your eyes. You will never know, dear Dorothy, what you were to the dull boy you bore with; you will never know with what romance you filled my life, with what devotion, with what tenderness and honour. At night I lay awake and worshipped you; in my dreams I saw you, and you loved me; and you remember, when we told each other stories—you have not forgotten, dearest—that Princess Hawthorn that was still the heroine of mine: who was she? I was not bold enough to tell, but she was you! You, my virgin huntress, my Diana, my queen.

DOROTHY. O silence, silence—pity!

FENWICK. No, dear; neither for your sake nor mine will I be silenced. I have begun; I must go on and finish, and put fortune to the touch. It was from you I learned honour, duty, piety, and love. I am as you made me, and I exist but to reverence and serve you. Why else have I come here, the length of England, my heart burning higher every mile, my very horse a clog to me? why, but to ask you for my wife? Dorothy, you will not deny me.

DOROTHY. You have not asked me about this broken trinket?

FENWICK. Why should I ask? I love you.

DOROTHY. Yet I must tell you. Sit down. (She picks up the necklace, and stands looking at it. Then, breaking down.) O John, John, it's long since I left home.

FENWICK. Too long, dear love. The very trees will welcome you.

DOROTHY. Ay, John, but I no longer love you. The old Dorothy is dead, God pardon her!

FENWICK. Dorothy, who is the man?

DOROTHY. O poor Dorothy! O poor dead Dorothy! John, you found me breaking this: me, your Diana of the Fells, the Diana of your old romance by Edenside. Diana—O what a name for me! Do you see this trinket? It is a chapter in my life. A chapter, do I say? my whole life, for there is none to follow. John, you must bear with me, you must help me. I have that to tell—there is a secret—I have a secret, John—O, for God's sake, understand. That Diana you revered—O John, John, you must never speak of love to me again.

FENWICK. What do you say? How dare you?

DOROTHY. John, it is the truth. Your Diana, even she, she whom you so believed in, she who so believed in herself, came out into the world only to be broken. I met, here at the Wells, a man—why should I tell you his name? I met him, and I loved him. My heart was all his own; yet he was not content with that: he must intrigue to catch me, he must bribe my maid with this. (Throws the necklace on the table.) Did he love me? Well, John, he said he did; and be it so! He loved, he betrayed, and he has left me.

FENWICK. Betrayed?

DOROTHY. Ay, even so; I was betrayed. The fault was mine that I forgot our innocent youth, and your honest love.

FENWICK. Dorothy, O Dorothy!

DOROTHY. Yours is the pain; but, O John, think it is for your good. Think in England how many true maids may be waiting for your love, how many that can bring you a whole heart, and be a noble mother to your children, while your poor Diana, at the first touch, has proved all frailty. Go, go and be happy, and let me be patient. I have sinned.

FENWICK. By God, I'll have his blood.

DOROTHY. Stop! I love him. (Between FENWICK and door, C.)

FENWICK. What do I care? I loved you too. Little he thought of that, little either of you thought of that. His blood—I'll have his blood!

DOROTHY. You shall never know his name.

FENWICK. Know it? Do you think I cannot guess? Do you think I had not heard he followed you. Do you think I had not suffered—O suffered! George Austin is the man. Dear shall he pay it!

DOROTHY (at his feet). Pity me; spare me, spare your Dorothy! I love him—love him—love him!

FENWICK. Dorothy, you have robbed me of my happiness, and now you would rob me of my revenge.

DOROTHY. I know it; and shall I ask, and you not grant?

FENWICK (raising her). No, Dorothy, you shall ask nothing, nothing in vain from me. You ask his life; I give it you, as I would give you my soul; as I would give you my life, if I had any left. My life is done; you have taken it. Not a hope, not an end; not even revenge. (He sits.) Dorothy, you see your work.

DOROTHY. O God, forgive me.

FENWICK. Ay, Dorothy, He will, as I do.

DOROTHY. As you do? Do you forgive me, John?

FENWICK. Ay, more than that, poor soul. I said my life was done, I was wrong; I have still a duty. It is not in vain you taught me; I shall still prove to you that it was not in vain. You shall soon find that I am no backward friend. Farewell.

ACT II.

MUSICAL INDUCTION: 'The Lass of Richmond Hill.'

The Stage represents George Austin's dressing-room. Elaborate toilet-table, R., with chair; a cheval glass so arranged as to correspond with glass on table. Breakfast-table, L., front. Door, L. The Beau is discovered at table, in dressing-grown, trifling with correspondence. MENTEITH is frothing chocolate.

SCENE I

AUSTIN, MENTEITH

MENTEITH. At the barber's, Mr. George, I had the pleasure of meeting two of the Dook's gentlemen.

AUSTIN. Well, and was his Royal Highness satisfied with his quarters?

MENTEITH. Quite so, Mr. George. Delighted, I believe.

AUSTIN. I am rejoiced to hear it. I wish I could say I was as pleased with my journey, Menteith. This is the first time I ever came to the Wells in another person's carriage; Duke or not, it shall be the last, Menteith.

MENTEITH. Ah, Mr. George, no wonder. And how many times have we made that journey back and forth?

AUSTIN. Enough to make us older than we look.

MENTEITH. To be sure, Mr. George, you do wear well.

AUSTIN. We wear well, Menteith.

MENTEITH. I hear, Mr. George, that Miss Musgrave is of the company.

AUSTIN. Is she so? Well, well! well, well!

MENTEITH. I've not seen the young lady myself, Mr. George; but the barber tells me she's looking poorly.

AUSTIN. Poorly?

MENTEITH. Yes, Mr. George, poorly was his word.

AUSTIN. Well, Menteith, I am truly sorry. She is not the first.

MENTEITH. Yes, Mr. George. (A bell. MENTEITH goes out, and re-enters with card.)

AUSTIN (with card). Whom have we here? Anthony Musgrave?

MENTEITH. A fine young man Mr. George; and with a look of the young lady, but not so gentlemanly.

AUSTIN. You have an eye, you have an eye. Let him in.

SCENE II

AUSTIN, MENTEITH, ANTHONY

AUSTIN. I am charmed to have this opportunity, Mr. Musgrave. You belong to my old corps, I think? And how does my good friend, Sir Frederick? I had his line; but like all my old comrades, he thinks last about himself, and gives me not of his news.

ANTHONY. I protest, sir, this is a very proud moment. Your name is still remembered in the regiment. (AUSTIN bows.) The Colonel—he keeps his health, sir, considering his age (AUSTIN bows again, and looks at MENTEITH)—tells us young men you were a devil of a fellow in your time.

AUSTIN. I believe I was—in my time. Menteith, give Mr. Musgrave a dish of chocolate. So, sir, we see you at the Wells.

ANTHONY. I have but just alighted. I had but one thought, sir: to pay my respects to Mr. Austin. I have not yet kissed my aunt and sister.

AUSTIN. In my time—to which you refer—the ladies had come first.

ANTHONY. The women? I take you, sir. But then you see, a man's relatives don't count. And besides, Mr. Austin, between men of the world, I am fairly running away from the sex: I am positively in flight. Little Hortense of the Opera; you know; she sent her love to you. She's mad about me, I think. You never saw a creature so fond.

AUSTIN. Well, well, child! you are better here. In my time—to which you have referred—I knew the lady. Does she wear well?

ANTHONY. I beg your pardon, sir!

AUSTIN. No offence, child, no offence. She was a very lively creature. But you neglect your chocolate I see?

ANTHONY. We don't patronise it, Mr. Austin; we haven't for some years: the service has quite changed since your time. You'd be surprised.

AUSTIN. Doubtless. I am.

ANTHONY. I assure you, sir, I and Jack Bosbury of the Fifty-Second—

AUSTIN. The Hampshire Bosburys?—

ANTHONY. I do not know exactly, sir. I believe he is related.

AUSTIN. Or perhaps—I remember a Mr. Bosbury, a cutter of coats. I have the vanity to believe I formed his business.

ANTHONY. I—I hope not, sir. But as I was saying, I and this Jack Bosbury, and the Brummagem Bantam—a very pretty light-weight, sir—drank seven bottles of Burgundy to the three of us inside the eighty minutes. Jack, sir, was a little cut; but me and the Bantam went out and finished the evening on hot gin. Life, sir, life! Tom Cribb was with us. He spoke of you, too, Tom did: said you'd given him a wrinkle for his second fight with the black man. No, sir, I assure you, you're not forgotten.

AUSTIN (bows). I am pleased to learn it. In my time, I had an esteem for Mr. Cribb.

ANTHONY. O come, sir! but your time cannot be said to be over.

AUSTIN. Menteith, you hear?

MENTEITH. Yes, Mr. George.

ANTHONY. The Colonel told me that you liked to shake an elbow. Your big main, sir, with Lord Wensleydale, is often talked about. I hope I may have the occasion to sit down with you. I shall count it an honour, I assure you.

AUSTIN. But would your aunt, my very good friend, approve?

ANTHONY. Why, sir, you do not suppose I am in leading-strings?

AUSTIN. You forget, child: a family must hang together. When I was young—in my time—I was alone; and what I did concerned myself. But a youth who has—as I think you have—a family of ladies to protect, must watch his honour, child, and preserve his fortune. You have no commands from Sir Frederick?

ANTHONY. None, sir, none.

AUSTIN. Shall I find you this noon upon the Pantiles? . . . I shall be charmed. Commend me to your aunt and your fair sister. Menteith?

MENTEITH. Yes, Mr. George. (Shows Anthony out.)

SCENE III

AUSTIN, MENTEITH, returning

AUSTIN. Was I ever like that, Menteith?

MENTEITH. No, Mr. George, you was always a gentleman.

AUSTIN. Youth, my good fellow, youth.

MENTEITH. Quite so, Mr. George.

AUSTIN. Well, Menteith, we cannot make no mend. We cannot play the jockey with Time. Age is the test: of wine, Menteith, and men.

MENTEITH. Me and you and the old Hermitage, Mr. George, he-he!

AUSTIN. And the best of these, the Hermitage. But come: we lose our day. Help me off with this. (MENTEITH takes off AUSTIN'S dressing-gown; AUSTIN passes R. to dressing-table, and takes up first cravat.)

AUSTIN. Will the hair do, Menteith?

MENTEITH. Never saw it lay better, Mr. George. (AUSTIN proceeds to wind first cravat. A bell: exit MENTEITH. AUSTIN drops first cravat in basket and takes second.)

AUSTIN (winding and singing)—

'I'd crowns resign
To call her mine,
Sweet Lass of Richmond Hill!'

(Second cravat a failure. Re-enter MENTEITH with card.) Fenwick? of Allonby Shaw? A good family, Menteith, but I don't know the gentleman. (Lays down card, and takes up third cravat.) Send him away with every consideration.

MENTEITH. To be sure, Mr. George. (He goes out. Third cravat a success. Re-enter MENTEITH.) He says, Mr. George, that he has an errand from Miss Musgrave.

AUSTIN (with waistcoat). Show him in, Menteith, at once. (Singing and fitting waistcoat at glass)—

'I'd crowns resign
To call her mine,
Sweet Lass of Richmond Hill!'

SCENE IV

AUSTIN, R. to him MENTEITH and FENWICK

MENTEITH (announcing). Mr. Fenwick, Mr. George.

AUSTIN. At the name of Miss Musgrave, my doors fly always open.

FENWICK. I believe, sir, you are acquainted with my cousin, Richard Gaunt?

AUSTIN. The county member? An old and good friend. But you need not go so far afield: I know your good house of Allonby Shaw since the days of the Black Knight. We are, in fact, and at a very royal distance, cousins.

FENWICK. I desired, sir, from the nature of my business, that you should recognise me for a gentleman.

AUSTIN. The preliminary, sir, is somewhat grave.

FENWICK. My business is both grave and delicate.

AUSTIN. Menteith, my good fellow. (Exit MENTEITH.) Mr. Fenwick, honour me so far as to be seated. (They sit.) I await your pleasure.

FENWICK. Briefly, sir, I am come, not without hope, to appeal to your good heart.

AUSTIN. From Miss Musgrave?

FENWICK. No, sir, I abused her name, and am here upon my own authority. Upon me the consequence.

AUSTIN. Proceed

FENWICK. Mr. Austin, Dorothy Musgrave is the oldest and dearest of my friends, is the lady whom for ten years it has been my hope to make my wife. She has shown me reason to discard that hope for another: that I may call her Mrs. Austin.

AUSTIN. In the best interests of the lady (rising) I question if you have been well inspired. You are aware, sir, that from such interference there is but one issue: to whom shall I address my friend?

FENWICK. Mr. Austin, I am here to throw myself upon your mercy. Strange as my errand is, it will seem yet more strange to you that I came prepared to accept at your hands any extremity of dishonour and not fight. The lady whom it is my boast to serve has honoured me with her commands. These are my law, and by these your life is sacred.

AUSTIN. Then, sir (with his hand upon the bell), his conversation becomes impossible. You have me at too gross a disadvantage; and, as you are a gentleman and respect another, I would suggest that you retire.

FENWICK. Sir, you speak of disadvantage; think of mine. All my life long, with all the forces of my nature, I have loved this lady. I came here to implore her to be my wife, to be my queen; my saint she had been always! She was too noble to deceive me. She told me what you know. I will not conceal that my first mood was of anger: I would have killed you like a dog. But, Mr. Austin—bear with me awhile—I, on the threshold of my life, who have made no figure in the world, nor ever shall now, who had but one treasure, and have lost it—if I, abandoning revenge, trampling upon jealousy, can supplicate you to complete my misfortune—O Mr. Austin! you who have lived, you whose gallantry is beyond the insolence of a suspicion, you who are a man crowned and acclaimed, who are loved, and loved by such a woman—you who excel me in every point of advantage, will you suffer me to surpass you in generosity?

AUSTIN. You speak from the heart. (Sits.) What do you want with me?

FENWICK. Marry her.

AUSTIN. Mr. Fenwick, I am the older man. I have seen much of life, much of society, much of love. When I was young, it was expected of a gentleman to be ready with his hat to a lady, ready with his sword to a man; to honour his word and his king; to be courteous with his equals, generous to his dependants, helpful and trusty in friendship. But it was not asked of us to be quixotic. If I had married every lady by whom it is my fortune—not my merit—to have been distinguished, the Wells would scarce be spacious enough for my establishment. You see, sir, that while I respect your emotion, I am myself conducted by experience. And besides, Mr. Fenwick, is not love a warfare? has it not rules? have not our fair antagonists their tactics, their weapons, their place of arms? and is there not a touch of—pardon me the word! of silliness in one who, having fought, and having vanquished, sounds a parley, and capitulates to his own prisoner? Had the lady chosen, had the fortune of war been other, 'tis like she had been Mrs. Austin. Now I . . . You know the world.

FENWICK. I know, sir, that the world contains much cowardice. To find Mr. Austin afraid to do the right, this surprises me.

AUSTIN. Afraid, child?

FENWICK. Yes, sir, afraid. You know her, you know if she be worthy; and you answer me with—the world: the world which has been at your feet: the world which Mr. Austin knows so well how to value and is so able to rule.

AUSTIN. I have lived long enough, Mr. Fenwick, to recognise that the world is a great power. It can make; but it can break.

FENWICK. Sir, suffer me: you spoke but now of friendship, and spoke warmly. Have you forgotten Colonel Villiers?

AUSTIN. Mr. Fenwick, Mr. Fenwick, you forget what I have suffered.

FENWICK. O sir, I know you loved him. And yet, for a random word you quarrelled; friendship was weighed in vain against the world's code of honour; you fought, and your friend fell. I have heard from others how he lay long in agony, and how you watched and nursed him, and it was in your embrace he died. In God's name have you forgotten that? Was not this sacrifice enough? or must the world, once again, step between Mr. Austin and his generous heart?

AUSTIN. Good God, sir, I believe you are in the right; I believe, upon my soul I believe, there is something in what you say.

FENWICK. Something, Mr. Austin? O credit me, the whole difference betwixt good and evil.

AUSTIN. Nay, nay, but there you go too far. There are many kinds of good: honour is a diamond cut in a thousand facets, and with the true fire in each. Thus, and with all our differences, Mr. Fenwick, you and I can still respect, we can still admire each other.

FENWICK. Bear with me still, sir, if I ask you what is the end of life but to excel in generosity? To pity the weak, to comfort the afflicted, to right where we have wronged, to be brave in reparation—these noble elements you have; for of what besides is the fabric of your dealing with Colonel Villiers? That is man's chivalry to man. Yet to a suffering woman—a woman feeble, betrayed, unconsoled—you deny your clemency, you refuse your aid, you proffer injustice for atonement. Nay, you are so disloyal to yourself that you can choose to be ungenerous and unkind. Where, sir, is the honour? What facet of the diamond is that?

AUSTIN. You forget, sir, you forget. But go on.

FENWICK. O sir, not I—not I but yourself forgets: George Austin forgets George Austin. A woman loved by him, betrayed by him, abandoned by him—that woman suffers; and a point of honour keeps him from his place at her feet. She has played and lost, and the world is with him if he deign to exact the stakes. Is that the Mr. Austin whom Miss Musgrave honoured with her trust? Then, sir, how miserably was she deceived!

AUSTIN. Child—child—

FENWICK. Mr. Austin, still bear with me, still follow me. O sir, will you not picture that dear lady's life? Her years how few, her error thus irreparable, what henceforth can be her portion but remorse, the consciousness of self-abasement, the shame of knowing that her trust was ill-bestowed? To think of it: this was a queen among women; and this—this is George Austin's work! Sir, let me touch your heart: let me prevail with you to feel that 'tis impossible.

AUSTIN. I am a gentleman. What do you ask of me?

FENWICK. To be the man she loved: to be clement where the world would have you triumph, to be of equal generosity with the vanquished, to be worthy of her sacrifice and of yourself.

AUSTIN. Mr. Fenwick, your reproof is harsh—

FENWICK (interrupting him). O sir, be, just be just!—

AUSTIN. But it is merited, and I thank you for its utterance. You tell me that the true victory comes when the fight is won: that our foe is never so noble nor so dangerous as when she is fallen, that the crowning triumph is that we celebrate over our conquering selves. Sir, you are right. Kindness, ay kindness after all. And with age, to become clement. Yes, ambition first; then, the rounded vanity—victory still novel; and last, as you say, the royal mood of the mature man; to abdicate for others . . . Sir, you touched me hard about my dead friend; still harder about my living duty; and I am not so young but I can take a lesson. There is my hand upon it: she shall be my wife.

FENWICK. Ah, Mr. Austin, I was sure of it.

AUSTIN. Then, sir, you were vastly mistaken. There is nothing of Beau Austin here. I have simply, my dear child, sate at the feet of Mr. Fenwick.

FENWICK. Ah, sir, your heart was counsellor enough.

AUSTIN. Pardon me. I am vain enough to be the judge: there are but two people in the world who could have wrought this change: yourself and that dear lady. (Touches bell.) Suffer me to dismiss you. One instant of toilet, and I follow. Will you do me the honour to go before, and announce my approach? (Enter MENTEITH.)

FENWICK. Sir, if my admiration—

AUSTIN. Dear child, the admiration is the other way. (Embraces him. MENTEITH shows him out.)

SCENE V

AUSTIN

AUSTIN. Upon my word, I think the world is getting better. We were none of us young men like that—in my time, to quote my future brother. (He sits down before the mirror.) Well, here ends Beau Austin. Paris, Rome, Vienna, London—victor everywhere: and now he must leave his bones in Tunbridge Wells. (Looks at his leg.) Poor Dolly Musgrave! a good girl after all, and will make me a good wife; none better. The last—of how many?—ay, and the best! Walks like Hebe. But still, here ends Beau Austin. Perhaps it's time. Poor Dolly—was she looking poorly? She shall have her wish. Well, we grow older, but we grow no worse.

SCENE VI

AUSTIN, MENTEITH

AUSTIN. Menteith, I am going to be married.

MENTEITH. Well, Mr. George, but I am pleased to hear it. Miss Musgrave is a most elegant lady.

AUSTIN. Ay, Mr. Menteith? and who told you the lady's name?

MENTEITH. Mr. George, you was always a gentleman.

AUSTIN. You mean I wasn't always? Old boy, you are in the right. This shall be a good change for both you and me. We have lived too long like a brace of truants: now is the time to draw about the fire. How much is left of the old Hermitage?

MENTEITH. Hard upon thirty dozen, Mr. George, and not a bad cork in the bin.

AUSTIN. And a mistress, Menteith, that's worthy of that wine.

MENTEITH. Mr. George, sir, she's worthy of you.

AUSTIN. Gad, I believe it. (Shakes hands with him.)

MENTEITH (breaking down). Mr. George, you've been a damned good master to me, and I've been a damned good servant to you; we've been proud of each other from the first; but if you'll excuse my plainness, Mr. George, I never liked you better than to-day.

AUSTIN. Cheer up, old boy, the best is yet to come. Get out the tongs, and curl me like a bridegroom. (Sits before dressing-glass; MENTEITH produces curling irons and plies them. AUSTIN sings)—

'I'd crowns resign
To call her mine,
Sweet Lass of Richmond Hill!'

ACT - CURTAIN DROP.

ACT III.

MUSICAL INDUCTION: the 'Minuet' from 'Don Giovanni'

The stage represents Miss Foster's lodging as in Act I.

SCENE I

DOROTHY, R., at tambour; ANTHONY, C., bestriding chair; MISS FOSTER, L.C.

ANTHONY. Yes, ma'am, I like my regiment: we are all gentlemen, from old Fred downwards, and all of a good family. Indeed, so are all my friends, except one tailor sort of fellow, Bosbury. But I'm done with him. I assure you, Aunt Evelina, we are Corinthian to the last degree. I wouldn't shock you ladies for the world—

MISS FOSTER. Don't mind me, my dear; go on.

ANTHONY. Really, ma'am, you must pardon me: I trust I understand what topics are to be avoided among females—And before my sister, too! A girl of her age!

DOROTHY. Why, you dear, silly fellow, I'm old enough to be your mother.

ANTHONY. My dear Dolly, you do not understand; you are not a man of the world. But, as I was going on to say, there is no more spicy regiment in the service.

MISS FOSTER. I am not surprised that it maintains its old reputation. You know, my dear (to DOROTHY), it was George Austin's regiment.

DOROTHY. Was it, aunt?

ANTHONY. Beau Austin? Yes, it was; and a precious dust they make about him still—a parcel of old frumps! That's why I went to see him. But he's quite extinct: he couldn't be Corinthian if he tried.

MISS FOSTER. I am afraid that even at your age George Austin held a very different position from the distinguished Anthony Musgrave.

ANTHONY. Come, ma'am, I take that unkindly. Of course I know what you're at: of course the old pût cut no end of a dash with the Duchess.

MISS FOSTER. My dear child, I was thinking of no such thing; that was immoral.

ANTHONY. Then you mean that affair at Brighton: when he cut the Prince about Perdita Robinson.

MISS FOSTER. No, I had forgotten it.

ANTHONY. O, well, I know—that duel! But look here, Aunt Evelina, I don't think you'd be much gratified after all if I were to be broke for killing my commanding officer about a quarrel at cards.

DOROTHY. Nobody asks you, Anthony, to imitate Mr. Austin. I trust you will set yourself a better model. But you may choose a worse. With all his faults, and all his enemies, Mr. Austin is a pattern gentleman! You would not ask a man to be braver, and there are few so generous. I cannot bear to hear him called in fault by one so young. Better judges, dear, are better pleased.

ANTHONY. Hey-day! what's this?

MISS FOSTER. Why, Dolly, this is April and May. You surprise me.

DOROTHY. I am afraid, indeed, madam, that you have much to suffer from my caprice. (She goes out, L.)

SCENE II

ANTHONY, MISS FOSTER

ANTHONY. What is the meaning of all this, ma'am? I don't like it.

MISS FOSTER. Nothing, child, that I know. You spoke of Mr. Austin, our dear friend, like a groom; and she, like any lady of taste, took arms in his defence.

ANTHONY. No, ma'am, that won't do. I know the sex. You mark my words, the girl has some confounded nonsense in her head, and wants looking after.

MISS FOSTER. In my presence, Anthony, I shall ask you to speak of Dorothy with greater respect. With your permission, your sister and I will continue to direct our own affairs. When we require the interference of so young and confident a champion, you shall know. (Curtsies, kisses her hand, and goes out, L.)

SCENE III

ANTHONY

ANTHONY. Upon my word, I think Aunt Evelina one of the most uncivil old women in the world. Nine weeks ago I came of age; and they still treat me like a boy. I'm a recognised Corinthian, too: take my liquor with old Fred, and go round with the Brummagem Bantam and Jack Bosb— . . . O damn Jack Bosbury. If his father was a tailor, he shall fight me for his ungentlemanly conduct. However, that's all one. What I want is to make Aunt Evelina understand that I'm not the man to be put down by an old maid who's been brought up in a work-basket, begad! I've had nothing but rebuffs all day. It's very remarkable. There was that man Austin, to begin with. I'll be hanged if I can stand him. I hear too much of him; and if I can only get a good excuse to put him to the door, I believe it would give Dorothy and all of us a kind of a position. After all, he's not a man to visit in the house of ladies: not when I'm away, at least. Nothing in it of course; but is he a man whose visits I can sanction?

SCENE IV

ANTHONY, BARBARA

BARBARA. Please, Mr. Anthony, Miss Foster said I was to show your room.

ANTHONY. Ha! Baby? Now, you come here. You're a girl of sense, I know.

BARBARA. La, Mr. Anthony, I hope I'm nothing of the kind.

ANTHONY. Come, come! that's not the tone I want: I'm serious. Does this man Austin come much about the house?

BARBARA. O Mr. Anthony, for shame! Why don't you ask Miss Foster?

ANTHONY. Now I wish you to understand: I'm the head of this family. It's my business to look after my sister's reputation, and my aunt's too, begad! That's what I'm here for: I'm their natural protector. And what I want you, Barbara Ridley, to understand—you whose fathers have served my fathers—is just simply this: if you've any common gratitude, you're bound to help me in the work. Now Barbara, you know me, and you know my Aunt Evelina. She's a good enough woman; I'm the first to say so. But who is she to take care of a young girl? She's ignorant of the world to that degree she believes in Beau Austin! Now you and I, Bab, who are not so high and dry, see through and through him; we know that a man like that is no fit company for any inexperienced girl.

BARBARA. O Mr. Anthony, don't say that. (Weeping.)

ANTHONY. Hullo! what's wrong?

BARBARA. Nothing that I know of. O Mr. Anthony, I don't think there can be anything.

ANTHONY. Think? Don't think? What's this?

BARBARA. O sir! I don't know, and yet I don't like it. Here's my beautiful necklace all broke to bits: she took it off my very neck, and gave me her birthday pearls instead; and I found it afterwards on the table, all smashed to pieces; and all she wanted it for was to take and break it. Why that? It frightens me, Mr. Anthony, it frightens me.

ANTHONY (with necklace). This? What has this trumpery to do with us?

BARBARA. He gave it me: that's why she broke it.

ANTHONY. He? who?

BARBARA. Mr. Austin did; and I do believe I should not have taken it, Mr. Anthony, but I thought no harm, upon my word of honour. He was always here: that was six months ago; and indeed, indeed, I thought they were to marry. How would I think else with a born lady like Miss Dorothy?

ANTHONY. Why, Barbara, God help us all, what's this? You don't mean to say that there was—

BARBARA. Here it is, as true as true: they were going for a jaunt; and Miss Foster had her gout; and I was to go with them; and he told me to make-believe I was ill; and I did; and I stayed at home; and he gave me that necklace; and they went away together; and, oh dear! I wish I'd never been born.

ANTHONY. Together? he and Dolly? Good Lord! my sister! And since then?

BARBARA. We haven't seen him from that day to this, the wicked villain; and, Mr. Anthony, he hasn't so much as written the poor dear a word.

ANTHONY. Bab, Bab, Bab, this is a devil of a bad business; this is a cruel bad business, Baby; cruel upon me, cruel upon all of us; a family like mine. I'm a young man, Barbara, to have this delicate affair to manage; but, thank God, I'm Musgrave to the bone. He bribed a servant-maid, did he? I keep his bribe; it's mine now; dear bought, by George! He shall have it in his teeth. Shot Colonel Villiers, did he? we'll see how he faces Anthony Musgrave. You're a good girl, Barbara; so far you've served the family. You leave this to me. And, hark ye, dry your eyes and hold your tongue: I'll have no scandal raised by you.

BARBARA. I do hope, sir, you won't use me against Miss Dorothy.

ANTHONY. That's my affair; your business is to hold your tongue. Miss Dorothy has made her bed and must lie on it. Here's Jack Fenwick. You can go.

SCENE V

ANTHONY, FENWICK

ANTHONY. Jack Fenwick, is that you? Come here, my boy. Jack, you've given me many a thrashing, and I deserved 'em; and I'll not see you made a fool of now. George Austin is a damned villain, and Dorothy Musgrave is no girl for you to marry: God help me that I should have to say it.

FENWICK. Good God, who told you?

ANTHONY. Ay, Jack; it's hard on me, Jack. But you'll stand my friend in spite of this, and you'll take my message to the man, won't you? For it's got to come to blood, Jack: there's no way out of that. And perhaps your poor friend will fall, Jack; think of that: like Villiers. And all for an unworthy sister.

FENWICK. Now, Anthony Musgrave, I give you fair warning; see you take it: one word more against your sister, and we quarrel.

ANTHONY. You let it slip yourself, Jack: you know yourself she's not a virtuous girl.

FENWICK. What do you know of virtue, whose whole boast is to be vicious? How dare you draw conclusions? Dolt and puppy! you can no more comprehend that angel's excellencies than she can stoop to believe in your vices. And you talk morality? Anthony, I'm a man who has been somewhat roughly tried: take care.

ANTHONY. You don't seem able to grasp the situation, Jack. It's very remarkable; I'm the girl's natural protector; and you should buckle-to and help, like a friend of the family. And instead of that, begad! you turn on me like all the rest.

FENWICK. Now mark me fairly: Mr. Austin follows at my heels; he comes to offer marriage to your sister—that is all you know, and all you shall know; and if by any misplaced insolence of yours this marriage should miscarry, you have to answer, not to Mr. Austin only, but to me.

ANTHONY. It's all a most discreditable business, and I don't see how you propose to better it by cutting my throat. Of course if he's going to marry her, it's a different thing; but I don't believe he is, or he'd have asked me. You think me a fool? Well see they marry, or they'll find me a dangerous fool.

SCENE VI

To these, AUSTIN, BARBARA announcing.

BARBARA. Mr. Austin. (She shows AUSTIN in, and retires.)

AUSTIN. You will do me the justice to acknowledge, Mr. Fenwick, that I have been not long delayed by my devotion to the Graces.

ANTHONY. So, sir, I find you in my house—

AUSTIN. And charmed to meet you again. It went against my conscience to separate so soon. Youth, Mr. Musgrave, is to us older men a perpetual refreshment.

ANTHONY. You came here, sir, I suppose, upon some errand?

AUSTIN. My errand, Mr. Musgrave, is to your fair sister. Beauty, as you know, comes before valour.

ANTHONY. In my own house, and about my own sister, I presume I have the right to ask for something more explicit.

AUSTIN. The right, my dear sir, is beyond question; but it is one, as you were going on to observe, on which no gentleman insists.

FENWICK. Anthony, my good fellow, I think we had better go.

ANTHONY. I have asked a question.

AUSTIN. Which I was charmed to answer, but which, on repetition, might begin to grow distasteful.

ANTHONY. In my own house—

FENWICK. For God's sake, Anthony!

AUSTIN. In your aunt's house, young gentleman, I shall be careful to refrain from criticism. I am come upon a visit to a lady: that visit I shall pay; when you desire (if it be possible that you desire it) to resume this singular conversation, select some fitter place. Mr. Fenwick, this afternoon, may I present you to his Royal Highness?

ANTHONY. Why, sir, I believe you must have misconceived me. I have no wish to offend: at least at present.

AUSTIN. Enough, sir. I was persuaded I had heard amiss. I trust we shall be friends.

FENWICK. Come, Anthony, come: here is your sister.

(As FENWICK and ANTHONY go out, C., enter DOROTHY, L.)

SCENE VII

AUSTIN, DOROTHY

DOROTHY. I am told, Mr. Austin, that you wish to see me.

AUSTIN. Madam, can you doubt of that desire? can you question my sincerity?

DOROTHY. Sir, between you and me these compliments are worse than idle: they are unkind. Sure, we are alone!

AUSTIN. I find you in an hour of cruelty, I fear. Yet you have condescended to receive this poor offender; and having done so much, you will not refuse to give him audience.

DOROTHY. You shall have no cause, sir, to complain of me. I listen.

AUSTIN. My fair friend, I have sent myself—a poor ambassador—to plead for your forgiveness. I have been too long absent; too long, I would fain hope, madam, for you; too long for my honour and my love. I am no longer, madam, in my first youth; but I may say that I am not unknown. My fortune, originally small, has not suffered from my husbandry. I have excellent health, an excellent temper, and the purest ardour of affection for your person. I found not on my merits, but on your indulgence. Miss Musgrave, will you honour me with your hand in marriage?

DOROTHY. Mr. Austin, if I thought basely of marriage, I should perhaps accept your offer. There was a time, indeed, when it would have made me proudest among women. I was the more deceived, and have to thank you for a salutary lesson. You chose to count me as a cipher in your rolls of conquest; for six months you left me to my fate; and you come here to-day—prompted, I doubt not, by an honourable impulse—to offer this tardy reparation. No: it is too late.

AUSTIN. Do you refuse?

DOROTHY. Yours is the blame: we are no longer equal. You have robbed me of the right to marry any one but you; and do you think me, then, so poor in spirit as to accept a husband on compulsion?

AUSTIN. Dorothy, you loved me once.

DOROTHY. Ay, you will never guess how much: you will never live to understand how ignominious a defeat that conquest was. I loved and trusted you: I judged you by myself; think, then, of my humiliation, when, at the touch of trial, all your qualities proved false, and I beheld you the slave of the meanest vanity—selfish, untrue, base! Think, sir, what a humbling of my pride to have been thus deceived: to have taken for my idol such a commonplace imposture as yourself; to have loved—yes, loved—such a shadow, such a mockery of man. And now I am unworthy to be the wife of any gentleman; and you—look me in the face, George—are you worthy to be my husband?

AUSTIN. No, Dorothy, I am not. I was a vain fool; I blundered away the most precious opportunity; and my regret will be lifelong. Do me the justice to accept this full confession of my fault. I am here to-day to own and to repair it.

DOROTHY. Repair it? Sir you condescend too far.

AUSTIN. I perceive with shame how grievously I had misjudged you. But now, Dorothy, believe me, my eyes are opened. I plead with you, not as my equal, but as one in all ways better than myself. I admire you, not in that trivial sense in which we men are wont to speak of women, but as God's work: as a wise mind, a noble soul, and a most generous heart, from whose society I have all to gain, all to learn. Dorothy, in one word, I love you.

DOROTHY. And what, sir, has wrought this transformation? You knew me of old, or thought you knew me? Is it in six months of selfish absence that your mind has changed? When did that change begin? A week ago? Sure, you would have written! To-day? Sir, if this offer be anything more than fresh offence, I have a right to be enlightened.

AUSTIN. Madam, I foresaw this question. So be it: I respect, and I will not deceive you. But give me, first of all, a moment for defence. There are few men of my habits and position who would have done as I have done: sate at the feet of a young boy, accepted his lessons, gone upon his errand: fewer still, who would thus, at the crisis of a love, risk the whole fortune of the soul—love, gratitude, even respect. Yet more than that! For conceive how I respect you, if I, whose lifelong trade has been flattery, stand before you and make the plain confession of a truth that must not only lower me, but deeply wound yourself.

DOROTHY. What means—?

AUSTIN. Young Fenwick, my rival for your heart, he it was that sent me.

DOROTHY. He? O disgrace! He sent you! That was what he meant? Am I fallen so low? Am I your common talk among men? Did you dice for me? Did he kneel? O John, John, how could you! And you, Mr. Austin, whither have you brought me down? shame heaping upon shame—to what end! oh, to what end?

AUSTIN. Madam, you wound me: you look wilfully amiss. Sure, any lady in the land might well be proud to be loved as you are loved, with such nobility as Mr. Fenwick's, with such humility as mine. I came, indeed, in pity, in good-nature, what you will. (See, dearest lady, with what honesty I speak: if I win you, it shall be with the unblemished truth.) All that is gone. Pity? it is myself I pity. I offer you not love—I am not worthy. I ask, I beseech of you: suffer me to wait upon you like a servant, to serve you with my rank, my name, the whole devotion of my life. I am a gentleman—ay, in spite of my fault—an upright gentleman; and I swear to you that you shall order your life and mine at your free will. Dorothy, at your feet, in remorse, in respect, in love—O such love as I have never felt, such love as I derided—I implore, I conjure you to be mine!

DOROTHY. Too late! too late.

AUSTIN. No, no, not too late: not too late for penitence, not too late for love.

DOROTHY. Which do you propose? that I should abuse your compassion, or reward your treachery? George Austin, I have been your mistress, and I will never be your wife.

AUSTIN. Child, dear child, I have not told you all: there is worse still: your brother knows; the boy as good as told me. Dorothy, this is scandal at the door—O let that move you: for that, if not for my sake, for that, if not for love, trust me, trust me again.

DOROTHY. I am so much the more your victim: that is all, and shall that change my heart? The sin must have its wages. This, too, was done long ago: when you stooped to lie to me. The shame is still mine, the fault still yours.

AUSTIN. Child, child, you kill me: you will not understand. Can you not see? the lad will force me to a duel.

DOROTHY. And you will kill him? Shame after shame, threat upon threat. Marry me, or you are dishonoured; marry me, or your brother dies: and this is man's honour! But my honour and my pride are different. I will encounter all misfortune sooner than degrade myself by an unfaithful marriage. How should I kneel before the altar, and vow to reverence as my husband you, you who deceived me as my lover?

AUSTIN. Dorothy, you misjudge me cruelly; I have deserved it. You will not take me for your husband; why should I wonder? You are right. I have indeed filled your life with calamity: the wages, ay, the wages, of my sin are heavy upon you. But I have one more thing to ask of your pity; and O remember, child, who it is that asks it: a man guilty in your sight, void of excuse, but old, and very proud, and most unused to supplication. Dorothy Musgrave, will you forgive George Austin?

DOROTHY. O, George!

AUSTIN. It is the old name: that is all I ask, and more than I deserve. I shall remember, often remember, how and where it was bestowed upon me for the last time. I thank you, Dorothy, from my heart; a heart, child, that has been too long silent, but is not too old, I thank God! not yet too old, to learn a lesson and to accept a reproof. I will not keep you longer: I will go—I am so bankrupt in credit that I dare not ask you to believe in how much sorrow. But, Dorothy, my acts will speak for me with more persuasion. If it be in my power, you shall suffer no more through me: I will avoid your brother; I will leave this place, I will leave England, to-morrow; you shall be no longer tortured with the neighbourhood of your ungenerous lover. Dorothy, farewell!

SCENE VIII

DOROTHY; to whom, ANTHONY, L.

DOROTHY (on her knees, and reaching with her hands.) George, George! (Enter ANTHONY.)

ANTHONY. Ha! what are you crying for?

DOROTHY. Nothing, dear! (Rising.)

ANTHONY. Is Austin going to marry you?

DOROTHY. I shall never marry.

ANTHONY. I thought as much. You should have come to me.

DOROTHY. I know, dear, I know; but there was nothing to come about.

ANTHONY. It's a lie. You have disgraced the family. You went to John Fenwick: see what he has made of it! But I will have you righted: it shall be atoned in the man's blood.

DOROTHY. Anthony! And if I had refused him?

ANTHONY. You? refuse George Austin? You never had the chance.

DOROTHY. I have refused him.

ANTHONY. Dorothy, you lie. You would shield your lover; but this concerns not you only: it strikes my honour and my father's honour.

DOROTHY. I have refused him—refused him, I tell you—refused him. The blame is mine; are you so mad and wicked that you will not see?

ANTHONY. I see this: that man must die.

DOROTHY. He? never! You forget, you forget whom you defy; you run upon your death.

ANTHONY. Ah, my girl, you should have thought of that before. It is too late now.

DOROTHY. Anthony, if I beg you—Anthony, I have tried to be a good sister; I brought you up, dear, nursed you when you were sick, fought for you, hoped for you, loved you—think of it, think of the dear past, think of our home and the happy winter nights, the castles in the fire, the long shining future, the love that was to forgive and suffer always—O you will spare, you will spare me this.

ANTHONY. I will tell you what I will do, Dolly: I will do just what you taught me—my duty: that, and nothing else.

DOROTHY. O Anthony, you also, you to strike me! Heavens, shall I kill them—I—I, that love them, kill them! Miserable, sinful girl! George, George, thank God, you will be far away! O go, George, go at once!

ANTHONY. He goes the coward! Ay, is this more of your contrivance? Madam, you make me blush. But to-day at least I know where I can find him. This afternoon, on the Pantiles, he must dance attendance on the Duke of York. Already he must be there; and there he is at my mercy.

DOROTHY. Thank God, you are deceived: he will not fight. He promised me that; thank God I have his promise for that.

ANTHONY. Promise! Do you see this? (producing necklace) the thing he bribed your maid with? I shall dash it in his teeth before the Duke and before all Tunbridge. Promise, you poor fool? what promise holds against a blow? Get to your knees and pray for him; for, by the God above, if he has any blood in his body, one of us shall die before to-night. (He goes out.)

DOROTHY. Anthony, Anthony! . . . O my God, George will kill him.

Music: 'Chè farò,' as the drop falls.

ACT - CURTAIN DROP.

ACT IV.

MUSICAL INDUCTION: 'Gavotte;' 'Iphigénie en Aulide.'

GLUCK

The Stage represents the Pantiles: the alleys fronting the spectators in parallel lines. At the back, a stand of musicians, from which the 'Gavotte' is repeated on muted strings. The music continues nearly through Scene I. Visitors walking to and fro beneath the lines. A seat in front, L.

SCENE I

MISS FOSTER, BARBARA, MENTEITH; Visitors

MISS FOSTER (entering; escorted by MENTEITH, and followed by BARBARA). And so, Menteith, here you are once more. And vastly pleased I am to see you, my good fellow, not only for your own sake, but because you harbinger the Beau. (Sits, L.; MENTEITH standing over her.)

MENTEITH. Honoured madam, I have had the pleasure to serve Mr. George for more than thirty years. This is a privilege—a very great privilege. I have beheld him in the first societies, moving among the first rank of personages; and none, madam, none outshone him.

BARBARA. I assure you, madam, when Mr. Menteith took me to the play, he talked so much of Mr. Austin that I couldn't hear a word of Mr. Kean.

MISS FOSTER. Well, well, and very right. That was the old school of service, Barbara, which you would do well to imitate. This is a child, Menteith, that I am trying to form.

MENTEITH. Quite so, madam.

MISS FOSTER. And are we soon to see our princely guest, Menteith?

MENTEITH. His Royal Highness, madam? I believe I may say quite so. Mr. George will receive our gallant prince upon the Pantiles (looking at his watch) in, I should say, a matter of twelve minutes from now. Such, madam, is Mr. George's order of the day.

BARBARA. I beg your pardon, madam, I am sure, but are we really to see one of His Majesty's own brothers? That will be pure! O madam, this is better than Carlisle.

MISS FOSTER. The wood-note wild: a loyal Cumbrian, Menteith.

MENTEITH. Eh? Quite so, madam.

MISS FOSTER. When she has seen as much of the Royal Family as you, my good fellow, she will find it vastly less entertaining.

MENTEITH. Yes, madam, indeed; In these distinguished circles, life is but a slavery. None of the best set would relish Tunbridge without Mr. George; Tunbridge and Mr. George (if you'll excuse my plainness, madam) are in a manner of speaking identified; and indeed it was the Dook's desire alone that brought us here.

BARBARA. What? the Duke? O dear! was it for that?

MENTEITH. Though, to be sure, madam, Mr. George would always be charmed to find himself (bowing) among so many admired members of his own set.

MISS FOSTER. Upon my word, Menteith, Mr. Austin is as fortunate in his servant as his reputation.

MENTEITH. Quite so, madam. But let me observe that the opportunities I have had of acquiring a knowledge of Mr. George's character have been positively unrivalled. Nobody knows Mr. George like his old attendant. The goodness of that gentleman—but, madam, you will soon be equally fortunate, if, as I understand, it is to be a match.

MISS FOSTER. I hope, Menteith, you are not taking leave of your senses. Is it possible you mean my niece?

MENTEITH. Madam, I have the honour to congratulate you. I put a second curl in Mr. George's hair on purpose.

SCENE II

To these, AUSTIN. MENTEITH falls back, and AUSTIN takes his place in front of MISS FOSTER, his attitude a counterpart of MENTEITH'S.

AUSTIN. Madam, I hasten to present my homage.

MISS FOSTER. A truce to compliments! Menteith, your charming fellow there, has set me positively crazy. Dear George Austin, is it true? can it be true?

AUSTIN. Madam, if he has been praising your niece he has been well inspired. If he was speaking, as I spoke an hour ago myself, I wish, Miss Foster, that he had held his tongue. I have indeed offered myself to Miss Dorothy, and she, with the most excellent reason, has refused me.

MISS FOSTER. Is it possible? why, my dear George Austin . . . then I suppose it is John Fenwick after all!

AUSTIN. Not one of us is worthy.

MISS FOSTER. This is the most amazing circumstance. You take my breath away. My niece refuse George Austin? why, I give you my word, I thought she had adored you. A perfect scandal: it positively must not get abroad.

AUSTIN. Madam, for that young lady I have a singular regard. Judge me as tenderly as you can, and set it down, if you must, to an old man's vanity—for, Evelina, we are no longer in the heyday of our youth—judge me as you will: I should prefer to have it known.

MISS FOSTER. Can you? George Austin, you? My youth was nothing; I was a failure; but for you? no, George, you never can, you never must be old. You are the triumph of my generation, George, and of our old friendship too. Think of my first dance and my first partner. And to have this story—no, I could not bear to have it told of you.

AUSTIN. Madam, there are some ladies over whom it is a boast to have prevailed; there are others whom it is a glory to have loved. And I am so vain, dear Evelina, that even thus I am proud to link my name with that of Dorothy Musgrave.

MISS FOSTER. George, you are changed. I would not know you.

AUSTIN. I scarce know myself. But pardon me, dear friend (taking his watch), in less than four minutes our illustrious guest will descend amongst us; and I observe Mr. Fenwick, with whom I have a pressing business. Suffer me, dear Evelina!—

SCENE III

To these, FENWICK. MISS FOSTER remains seated, L. AUSTIN goes R. to FENWICK, whom he salutes with great respect

AUSTIN. Mr. Fenwick, I have played and lost. That noble lady, justly incensed at my misconduct, has condemned me. Under the burden of such a loss, may I console myself with the esteem of Mr. Fenwick?

FENWICK. She refused you? Pardon me, sir, but was the fault not yours?

AUSTIN. Perhaps to my shame, I am no novice, Mr. Fenwick; but I have never felt nor striven as to-day. I went upon your errand; but, you may trust me, sir, before I had done I found it was my own. Until to-day I never rightly valued her; sure, she is fit to be a queen. I have a remorse here at my heart to which I am a stranger. Oh! that was a brave life, that was a great heart that I have ruined.

FENWICK. Ay, sir, indeed.

AUSTIN. But, sir, it is not to lament the irretrievable that I intrude myself upon your leisure. There is something to be done, to save, at least to spare, that lady. You did not fail to observe the brother?

FENWICK. No, sir, he knows all; and being both intemperate and ignorant—

AUSTIN. Surely. I know. I have to ask you then to find what friends you can among this company; and if you have none, to make them. Let everybody hear the news. Tell it (if I may offer the suggestion) with humour: how Mr. Austin, somewhat upon the wane, but still filled with sufficiency, gloriously presumed and was most ingloriously set down by a young lady from the north: the lady's name a secret, which you will permit to be divined. The laugh—the position of the hero—will make it circulate;—you perceive I am in earnest;—and in this way I believe our young friend will find himself forestalled.

FENWICK. Mr. Austin, I would not have dared to ask so much of you; I will go further: were the positions changed, I should fear to follow your example.

AUSTIN. Child, child, you could not afford it.

SCENE IV

To there, the ROYAL DUKE, C.; then, immediately, ANTHONY, L. FENWICK crosses to MISS FOSTER, R. AUSTIN accosts the DUKE, C., in dumb show; the muted strings take up a new air, Mozart's 'Anglaise'; couples passing under the limes, and forming a group behind AUSTIN and the DUKE. ANTHONY in front, L., watches AUSTIN, who, as he turns from the DUKE, sees him, and comes forward with extended hand

AUSTIN. Dear child, let me present you to his Royal Highness.

ANTHONY (with necklace). Mr. Austin, do you recognise the bribe you gave my sister's maid?

AUSTIN. Hush, sir, hush! you forget the presence of the Duke.

ANTHONY. Mr. Austin, you are a coward and a scoundrel.

AUSTIN. My child, you will regret these words: I refuse your quarrel.

ANTHONY. You do? Take that. (He strikes AUSTIN on the mouth. At the moment of the blow—)

SCENE V

To these, DOROTHY, L. U. E. DOROTHY, unseen by AUSTIN, shrieks. Sensation. Music stops. Tableau

AUSTIN (recovering his composure). Your Royal Highness, suffer me to excuse the disrespect of this young gentleman. He has so much apology, and I have, I hope, so good a credit, as incline me to accept this blow. But I must beg of your Highness, and, gentlemen, all of you here present, to bear with me while I will explain what is too capable of misconstruction. I am the rejected suitor of this young gentleman's sister; of Miss Dorothy Musgrave: a lady whom I singularly honour and esteem; a word from whom (if I could hope that word) would fill my life with happiness. I was not worthy of that lady; when I was defeated in fair field, I presumed to make advances through her maid. See in how laughable a manner fate repaid me! The waiting-girl derided, the mistress denied, and now comes in this very ardent champion who publicly insults me. My vanity is cured; you will judge it right, I am persuaded, all of you, that I should accept my proper punishment in silence; you, my Lord Duke, to pardon this young gentleman; and you, Mr. Musgrave, to spare me further provocation, which I am determined to ignore.

DOROTHY (rushing forward, falling at AUSTIN'S knees, and seizing his hand). George, George, it was for me. My hero! take me! What you will!

AUSTIN (in an agony). My dear creature, remember that we are in public. (Raising her.) Your Royal Highness, may I present you Mrs. George Frederick Austin? (The Curtain falls on a few bars of the 'Lass of Richmond Hill.')

ADMIRAL GUINEA

DEDICATED WITH AFFECTION AND ESTEEM TO ANDREW LANG BY THE SURVIVORS OF THE WALRUS

SAVANNAH, this 27th day of September 1884

PERSONS REPRESENTED

JOHN GAUNT, called 'ADMIRAL GUINEA,' once Captain of the Slaver Arethusa.
ARETHUSA GAUNT, his Daughter.
DAVID PEW, a Blind Beggar, once Boatswain of the Arethusa
KIT FRENCH, a Privateersman.
MRS. DRAKE, Landlady of the Admiral Benbow Inn.

The Scene is laid in the neighbourhood of Barnstaple. The Time is about the year 1760. The action occupies part of a day and night.

NOTE.—Passages suggested for omission in representation are enclosed in square brackets, thus [ ].

ACT I.

The Stage represents a room in the Admiral Guinea's house: fireplace, arm-chair, and table with Bible, L., towards the front; door C., with window on each side, the window on the R., practicable; doors, R. and L., back; corner cupboard, a brass-strapped sea-chest fixed to the wall and floor, R.; cutlasses, telescopes, sextant, quadrant, a calendar, and several maps upon the wall; a ship clock; three wooden chairs; a dresser against wall, R. C.; on the chimney-piece the model of a brig and several shells. The centre bare of furniture. Through the widows and the door, which is open, green trees and a small field of sea.

SCENE I

ARETHUSA is discovered, dusting

ARETHUSA. Ten months and a week to-day! Now for a new mark. Since the last, the sun has set and risen over the fields and the pleasant trees at home, and on Kit's lone ship and the empty sea. Perhaps it blew; perhaps rained; (at the chart) perhaps he was far up here to the nor'ard, where the icebergs sail; perhaps at anchor among these wild islands of the snakes and buccaneers. O, you big chart, if I could see him sailing on you! North and South Atlantic; such a weary sight of water and no land; never an island for the poor lad to land upon. But still, God's there. (She takes down the telescope to dust it.) Father's spy-glass again; and my poor Kit perhaps with such another, sweeping the great deep!

SCENE II

ARETHUSA; to her, KIT, C. [He enters on tiptoe, and she does not see or hear him]

ARETHUSA (dusting telescope). At sea they have less dust at least: that's so much comfort.

KIT. Sweetheart, ahoy!

ARETHUSA. Kit!

KIT. Arethusa.

ARETHUSA. My Kit! Home again—O my love!—home again to me!

KIT. As straight as wind and tide could carry me!

ARETHUSA. O Kit, my dearest. O Kit—O! O!

KIT. Hey? Steady, lass: steady, I say. For goodness' sake, ease it off.

ARETHUSA. I will, Kit—I will. But you came so sudden.

KIT. I thought ten months of it about preparation enough.

ARETHUSA. Ten months and a week: you haven't counted the days as I have. Another day gone, and one day nearer to Kit: that has been my almanac. How brown you are! how handsome!

KIT. A pity you can't see yourself! Well, no, I'll never be handsome: brown I may be, never handsome. But I'm better than that, if the proverb's true; for I'm ten hundred thousand fathoms deep in love. I bring you a faithful sailor. What! you don't think much of that for a curiosity? Well, that's so: you're right; the rarity is in the girl that's worth it ten times over. Faithful? I couldn't help it if I tried! No, sweetheart, and I fear nothing: I don't know what fear is, but just of losing you. (Starting.) Lord, that's not the Admiral?

ARETHUSA. Aha, Mr. Dreadnought! you see you fear my father.

KIT. That I do. But, thank goodness, it's nobody. Kiss me: no, I won't kiss you: kiss me. I'll give you a present for that. See!

ARETHUSA. A wedding-ring!

KIT. My mother's. Will you take it?

ARETHUSA. Yes, will I—and give myself for it.

KIT. Ah, if we could only count upon your father! He's a man every inch of him; but he can't endure Kit French.

ARETHUSA. He hasn't learned to know you, Kit, as I have, nor yet do you know him. He seems hard and violent; at heart he is only a man overwhelmed with sorrow. Why else, when he looks at me and does not know that I observe him, should his face change, and fill with such tenderness, that I could weep to see him? Why, when he walks in his sleep, as he does almost every night, his eyes open and beholding nothing, why should he cry so pitifully on my mother's name? Ah, if you could hear him then, you would say yourself: here is a man that has loved; here is a man that will be kind to lovers.

KIT. Is that so? Ay, it's a hard thing to lose your wife; ay, that must cut the heart indeed. But for all that, my lass, your father is keen for the doubloons.

ARETHUSA. Right, Kit: and small blame to him. There is only one way to be honest, and the name of that is thrift.

KIT. Well, and that's my motto. I've left the ship; no more letter of marque for me. Good-bye to Kit French, privateersman's mate; and how-d'ye-do to Christopher, the coasting skipper. I've seen the very boat for me: I've enough to buy her, too; and to furnish a good house, and keep a shot in the locker for bad luck. So far, there's nothing to gainsay. So far it's hopeful enough; but still there's Admiral Guinea, you know—and the plain truth is that I'm afraid of him.

ARETHUSA. Admiral Guinea? Now Kit, if you are to be true lover of mine, you shall not use that name. His name is Captain Gaunt. As for fearing him, Kit French, you're not the man for me, if you fear anything but sin. He's a stern man because he's in the right.

KIT. He is a man of God; I am what he calls a child of perdition. I was a privateersman—serving my country, I say; but he calls it pirate. He is thrifty and sober; he has a treasure, they say, and it lies so near his heart that he tumbles up in his sleep to stand watch over it. What has a harum-scarum dog like me to expect from a man like him? He won't see I'm starving for a chance to mend; 'Mend,' he'll say; 'I'll be shot if you mend at the expense of my daughter;' and the worst of it is, you see, he'll be right.

ARETHUSA. Kit, if you dare to say that faint-hearted word again, I'll take my ring off. What are we here for but to grow better or grow worse? Do you think Arethusa French will be the same as Arethusa Gaunt?

KIT. I don't want her better.

ARETHUSA. Ah, but she shall be!

KIT. Hark, here he is! By George, it's neck or nothing now. Stand by to back me up.

SCENE III

To these, GAUNT, C.

KIT (with ARETHUSA'S hand). Captain Gaunt, I have come to ask you for your daughter.

GAUNT. Hum. (He sits in his chair, L.)

KIT. I love her, and she loves me, sir. I've left the privateering. I've enough to set me up and buy a tidy sloop—Jack Lee's; you know the boat, Captain; clinker built, not four years old, eighty tons burthen, steers like a child. I've put my mother's ring on Arethusa's finger; and if you'll give us your blessing, I'll engage to turn over a new leaf, and make her a good husband.

GAUNT. In whose strength, Christopher French?

KIT. In the strength of my good, honest love for her: as you did for her mother, and my father for mine. And you know, Captain, a man can't command the wind; but (excuse me, sir) he can always lie the best course possible, and that's what I'll do, so God help me.

GAUNT. Arethusa, you at least are the child of many prayers; your eyes have been unsealed; and to you the world stands naked, a morning watch for duration, a thing spun of cobwebs for solidity. In the presence of an angry God, I ask you: have you heard this man?

ARETHUSA. Father, I know Kit, and I love him.

GAUNT. I say it solemnly, this is no Christian union. To you, Christopher French, I will speak nothing of eternal truths: I will speak to you the language of this world. You have been trained among sinners who gloried in their sin: in your whole life you never saved one farthing; and now, when your pockets are full, you think you can begin, poor dupe, in your own strength. You are a roysterer, a jovial companion; you mean no harm—you are nobody's enemy but your own. No doubt you tell this girl of mine, and no doubt you tell yourself, that you can change. Christopher, speaking under correction, I defy you! You ask me for this child of many supplications, for this brand plucked from the burning: I look at you; I read you through and through; and I tell you—no! (Striking table with his fist.)

KIT. Captain Gaunt, if you mean that I am not worthy of her, I'm the first to say so. But, if you'll excuse me, sir, I'm a young man, and young men are no better'n they ought to be; it's known; they're all like that; and what's their chance? To be married to a girl like this! And would you refuse it to me? Why, sir, you yourself, when you came courting, you were young and rough; and yet I'll make bold to say that Mrs. Gaunt was a happy woman, and the saving of yourself into the bargain. Well, now, Captain Gaunt, will you deny another man, and that man a sailor, the very salvation that you had yourself?

GAUNT. Salvation, Christopher French, is from above.

KIT. Well, sir, that is so; but there's means, too; and what means so strong as the wife a man has to strive and toil for, and that bears the punishment whenever he goes wrong? Now, sir, I've spoke with your old shipmates in the Guinea trade. Hard as nails, they said, and true as the compass: as rough as a slaver, but as just as a judge. Well, sir, you hear me plead: I ask you for my chance; don't you deny it to me.

GAUNT. You speak of me? In the true balances we both weigh nothing. But two things I know: the depth of iniquity, how foul it is; and the agony with which a man repents. Not until seven devils were cast out of me did I awake; each rent me as it passed. Ay, that was repentance. Christopher, Christopher, you have sailed before the wind since first you weighed your anchor, and now you think to sail upon a bowline? You do not know your ship, young man: you will go to le'ward like a sheet of paper; I tell you so that know—I tell you so that have tried, and failed, and wrestled in the sweat of prayer, and at last, at last, have tasted grace. But, meanwhile, no flesh and blood of mine shall lie at the mercy of such a wretch as I was then, or as you are this day. I could not own the deed before the face of heaven if I sanctioned this unequal yoke. Arethusa, pluck off that ring from off your finger. Christopher French, take it, and go hence.

KIT. Arethusa, what do you say?

ARETHUSA. O Kit, you know my heart. But he is alone, and I am his only comfort; and I owe all to him; and shall I not obey my father? But, Kit, if you will let me, I will keep your ring. Go, Kit; go, and prove to my father that he was mistaken; go and win me. And O, Kit, if ever you should weary, come to me—no, do not come! but send a word—and I shall know all, and you shall have your ring. (GAUNT opens his Bible and begins to read.)

KIT. Don't say that, don't say such things to me; I sink or swim with you. (To GAUNT.) Old man, you've struck me hard; give me a good word to go with. Name your time; I'll stand the test. Give me a spark of hope, and I'll fight through for it. Say just this—'Prove I was mistaken,' and by George, I'll prove it.

GAUNT (looking up). I make no such compacts. Go, and swear not at all.

ARETHUSA. Go, Kit! I keep the ring.

SCENE IV

ARETHUSA, GAUNT

ARETHUSA. Father, what have we done that you should be so cruel?

GAUNT (laying down Bible, and rising). Do you call me cruel? You speak after the flesh. I have done you this day a service that you will live to bless me for upon your knees.

ARETHUSA. He loves me, and I love him: you can never alter that; do what you will, father, that can never change. I love him, I believe in him, I will be true to him.

GAUNT. Arethusa, you are the sole thing death has left me on this earth; and I must watch over your carnal happiness and your eternal weal. You do not know what this implies to me. Your mother—my Hester—tongue cannot tell, nor heart conceive the pangs she suffered. If it lies in me, your life shall not be lost on that same reef of an ungodly husband. (Goes out, C.)

SCENE V

ARETHUSA

ARETHUSA. I thought the time dragged long and weary when I knew that Kit was homeward bound, all the white sails a-blowing out towards England, and my Kit's face turned this way? (She begins to dust.) Sure, if my mother were here, she would understand and help us; she would understand a young maid's heart, though her own had never an ache; and she would love my Kit. (Putting back the telescope.) To think she died: husband and child—and so much love—she was taken from them all. Ah, there is no parting but the grave! And Kit and I both live, and both love each other; and here am I cast down? O, Arethusa, shame! And your love home from the deep seas, and loving you still; and the sun shining; and the world all full of hope? O, hope, you're a good word!

SCENE VI

GAUNT

ARETHUSA; to her, PEW

PEW (singing without)—

'Time for us to go!
Time for us to go!
And we'll keep the brig three pints away,
For it's time for us to go.'

ARETHUSA. Who comes here? a seaman by his song, and father out! (She tries the air) 'Time for us to go!' It sounds a wild kind of song. (Tap-tap; PEW passes the window.) O, what a face—and blind!

PEW (entering). Kind Christian friends, take pity on a poor blind mariner, as lost his precious sight in the defence of his native country, England, and God bless King George!

ARETHUSA. What can I do for you, sailor?

PEW. Good Christian lady, help a poor blind mariner to a mouthful of meat. I've served His Majesty in every quarter of the globe; I've spoke with 'Awke and glorious Anson, as I might with you; and I've tramped it all night long, upon my sinful feet, and with a empty belly.

ARETHUSA. You shall not ask bread and be denied by a sailor's daughter and a sailor's sweetheart; and when my father returns he shall give you something to set you on your road.

PEW. Kind and lovely lady, do you tell me that you are in a manner of speaking alone? or do my ears deceive a poor blind seaman?

ARETHUSA. I live here with my father, and my father is abroad.

PEW. Dear, beautiful, Christian lady, tell a poor blind man your honoured name, that he may remember it in his poor blind prayers.

ARETHUSA. Sailor, I am Arethusa Gaunt.

PEW. Sweet lady, answer a poor blind man one other question: are you in a manner of speaking related to Cap'n John Gaunt? Cap'n John as in the ebony trade were known as Admiral Guinea?

ARETHUSA. Captain John Gaunt is my father.

PEW (dropping the blind man's whine). Lord, think of that now! They told me this was where he lived, and so it is. And here's old Pew, old David Pew, as was the Admiral's own bo'sun, colloguing in his old commander's parlour, with his old commander's gal (seizes ARETHUSA). Ah, and a bouncer you are, and no mistake.

ARETHUSA. Let me go! how dare you?

PEW. Lord love you, don't you struggle, now, don't you. (She escapes into front R. corner, where he keeps her imprisoned.) Ah, well, we'll get you again, my lovely woman. What a arm you've got—great god of love—and a face like a peach! I'm a judge, I am. (She tries to escape; he stops her.) No, you don't; O, I can hear a flea jump! [But it's here where I miss my deadlights. Poor old Pew; him as the ladies always would have for their fancy man and take no denial; here you are with your

Commander's daughter close aboard, and you can't so much as guess the colour of her lovely eyes. (Singing)—

'Be they black like ebony;   Or be they blue like to the sky.'

Black like the Admiral's? or blue like his poor dear wife's? Ah, I was fond of that there woman, I was: the Admiral was jealous of me.] Arethusa, my dear,—my heart, what a 'and and arm you have got; I'll dream o' that 'and and arm, I will!—but as I was a-saying, does the Admiral ever in a manner of speaking refer to his old bo'sun David Pew? him as he fell out with about the black woman at Lagos, and almost slashed the shoulder off of him one morning before breakfast?

ARETHUSA. You leave this house.

PEW. Hey? (he crosses and seizes her again) Don't you fight, my lovely one: now don't make old blind Pew forget his manners before a female. What! you will? Stop that, or I'll have the arm right out of your body. (He gives her arm a wrench.)

ARETHUSA. O! help, help!

PEW. Stash your patter, damn you. (ARETHUSA gives in.) Ah, I thought it: Pew's way, Pew's way. Now, look you here, my lovely woman. If you sling in another word that isn't in answer to my questions, I'll pull your j'ints out one by one. Where's the Commander?

ARETHUSA. I have said: he is abroad.

PEW. When's he coming aboard again?

ARETHUSA. At any moment.

PEW. Does he keep his strength?

ARETHUSA. You'll see when he returns. (He wrenches her arm again.) Ah!

PEW. Is he still on piety?

ARETHUSA. O, he is a Christian man!

PEW. A Christian man, is he? Where does he keep his rum?

ARETHUSA. Nay, you shall steal nothing by my help.

PEW. No more I shall (becoming amorous). You're a lovely woman, that's what you are; how would you like old Pew for a sweetheart, hey? He's blind, is Pew, but strong as a lion; and the sex is his 'ole delight. Ah, them beautiful, beautiful lips! A kiss! Come!

ARETHUSA. Leave go, leave go!

PEW. Hey? you would?

ARETHUSA. Ah! (She thrusts him down, and escapes to door, R.)

SCENE VII

PEW (picking himself up). Ah, she's a bouncer, she is! Where's my stick? That's the sort of female for David Pew. Didn't she fight? and didn't she struggle? and shouldn't I like to twist her lovely neck for her? Pew's way with 'em all: the prettier they was, the uglier he were to 'em. Pew's way: a way he had with him; and a damned good way too. (Listens at L. door.) That's her bedroom, I reckon; and she's double-locked herself in. Good again: it's a crying mercy the Admiral didn't come in. But you always loses your 'ed, Pew, with a female: that's what charms 'em. Now for business. The front door. No bar; only a big lock (trying keys from his pocket). Key one; no go. Key two; no go. Key three; ah, that does it. Ah! (feeling key) him with the three wards and the little 'un: good again! Now if I could only find a mate in this rotten country 'amlick: one to be eyes to me; I can steer, but I can't conn myself, worse luck! If I could only find a mate! And to-night, about three bells in the middle watch, old Pew will take a little cruise, and lay aboard his ancient friend the Admiral; or, barring that, the Admiral's old sea-chest—the chest he kept the shiners in aboard the brig. Where is it, I wonder? in his berth, or in the cabin here? It's big enough, and the brass bands is plain to feel by. (Searching about with stick.) Dresser—chair—(knocking his head on the cupboard.) Ah!—O, corner cupboard. Admiral's chair—Admiral's table—Admiral's—hey! what's this?—a book—sheepskin—smells like a 'oly Bible. Chair (his stick just avoids the chest). No sea-chest. I must have a mate to see for me, to see for old Pew: him as had eyes like a eagle! Meanwhile, rum. Corner cupboard, of course (tap-tapping). Rum—rum—rum. Hey? (He listens.) Footsteps. Is it the Admiral? (With the whine.) Kind Christian friends—

SCENE VIII

PEW; to him GAUNT

GAUNT. What brings you here?

PEW. Cap'n, do my ears deceive me? or is this my old commander?

GAUNT. My name is John Gaunt. Who are you, my man, and what's your business?

PEW. Here's the facks, so help me. A lovely female in this house was Christian enough to pity the poor blind; and lo and belold! who should she turn out to be but my old commander's daughter! 'My dear,' says I to her, 'I was the Admiral's own particular bo'sun.'—'La, sailor,' she says to me, 'how glad he'll be to see you!'—'Ah,' says I, 'won't he just—that's all.'—'I'll go and fetch him,' she says; 'you make yourself at 'ome.' And off she went; and, Commander, here I am.

GAUNT (sitting down). Well?

PEW. Well, Cap'n?

GAUNT. What do you want?

PEW. Well, Admiral, in a general way, what I want in a manner of speaking is money and rum. (A pause.)

GAUNT. David Pew, I have known you a long time.

PEW. And so you have aboard the old Arethusa; and you don't seem that cheered up as I'd looked for, with an old shipmate dropping in, one as has been seeking you two years and more—and blind at that. Don't you remember the old chantie?

'Time for us to go,
Time for us to go,
And when we'd clapped the hatches on,
'Twas time for us to go.

What a note you had to sing, what a swaller for a pannikin of rum, and what a fist for the shiners! Ah, Cap'n, they didn't call you Admiral Guinea for nothing. I can see that old sea-chest of yours—her with the brass bands, where you kept your gold dust and doubloons: you know! I can see her as well this minute as though you and me was still at it playing pût on the lid of her . . . You don't say nothing, Cap'n? . . . Well, here it is: I want money and I want rum. You don't know what it is to want rum, you don't: it gets to that p'int, that you would kill a 'ole ship's company for just one guttle of it. What? Admiral Guinea, my old Commander, go back on poor old Pew? and him high and dry? [Not you! When we had words over the negro lass at Lagos, what did you do? fair dealings was your word: fair as between man and man; and we had it out with p'int and edge on Lagos sands. And you're not going back on your word to me, now I'm old and blind? No, no! belay that, I say. Give me the old motto: Fair dealings, as between man and man.]

GAUNT. David Pew, it were better for you that you were sunk in fifty fathom. I know your life; and first and last, it is one broadside of wickedness. You were a porter in a school, and beat a boy to death; you ran for it, turned slaver, and shipped with me, a green hand. Ay, that was the craft for you: that was the right craft, and I was the right captain; there was none worse that sailed to Guinea. Well, what came of that? In five years' time you made yourself the terror and abhorrence of your messmates. The worst hands detested you; your captain—that was me, John Gaunt, the chief of sinners—cast you out for a Jonah. [Who was it stabbed the Portuguese and made off inland with his miserable wife? Who, raging drunk on rum, clapped fire to the baracoons and burned the poor soulless creatures in their chains?] Ay, you were a scandal to the Guinea coast, from Lagos down to Calabar? and when at last I sent you ashore, a marooned man—your shipmates, devils as they were, cheering and rejoicing to be quit of you—by heaven, it was a ton's weight off the brig!

PEW. Cap'n Gaunt, Cap'n Gaunt, these are ugly words.

GAUNT. What next? You shipped with Flint the Pirate. What you did then I know not; the deep seas have kept the secret: kept it, ay, and will keep against the Great Day. God smote you with blindness, but you heeded not the sign. That was His last mercy; look for no more. To your knees, man, and repent! Pray for a new heart; flush out your sins with tears; flee while you may from the terrors of the wrath to come.

PEW. Now, I want this clear: Do I understand that you're going back on me, and you'll see me damned first?

GAUNT. Of me you shall have neither money nor strong drink: not a guinea to spend in riot; not a drop to fire your heart with devilry.

PEW. Cap'n, do you think it wise to quarrel with me? I put it to you now, Cap'n, fairly, as between man and man—do you think it wise?

GAUNT. I fear nothing. My feet are on the Rock. Begone! (He opens the Bible and begins to read.)

PEW (after a pause). Well, Cap'n, you know best, no doubt; and David Pew's about the last man, though I says it, to up and thwart an old Commander. You've been 'ard on David Pew, Cap'n: 'ard on the poor blind; but you'll live to regret it—ah, my Christian friend, you'll live to eat them words up. But there's no malice here: that ain't Pew's way; here's a sailor's hand upon it . . . You don't say nothing? (GAUNT turns a page.) Ah, reading, was you? Reading, by thunder! Well, here's my respecks (singing)—

'Time for us to go,
Time for us to go,
When the money's out, and the liquor's done,
Why, it's time for us to go.

(He goes tapping up to door, turns on the threshold, and listens. GAUNT turns a page. PEW, with a grimace, strikes his hand upon the pocket with the keys, and goes.)

ACT - CURTAIN DROP.

ACT II.

The Stage represents the parlour of the 'Admiral Benbow' inn. Fire-place, R., with high-backed settles on each side; in front of these, and facing the audience, R., a small table laid with a cloth. Tables, L., with glasses, pipes, etc. Broadside ballads on the wall. Outer door of inn, with the half-door in L., corner back; door, R., beyond the fire-place; window with red half-curtains; spittons; candles on both the front tables; night without.

SCENE I

PEW; afterwards MRS. DRAKE, out and in

PEW (entering). Kind Christian friends—(listening; then dropping the whine.) Hey? nobody! Hey? A grog-shop not two cable-lengths from the Admiral's back-door, and the Admiral not there? I never knew a seaman brought so low: he ain't but the bones of the man he used to be. Bear away for the New Jerusalem, and this is what you run aground on, is it? Good again; but it ain't Pew's way; Pew's way is rum.—Sanded floor. Rum is his word, and rum his motion.—Settle—chimbley—settle again—spittoon—table rigged for supper. Table-glass. (Drinks heeltap.) Brandy and water; and not enough of it to wet your eye; damn all greediness, I say. Pot (drinks), small beer—a drink that I ab'or like bilge! What I want is rum. (Calling, and rapping with stick on table.) Halloa, there! House, ahoy!

MRS. DRAKE (without). Coming, sir, coming. (She enters, R.) What can I do—? (Seeing PEW.) Well I never did! Now, beggar-man, what's for you?

[PEW. Rum, ma'am, rum; and a bit o' supper.

MRS. DRAKE. And a bed to follow, I shouldn't wonder!

PEW. And a bed to follow: if you please.]

MRS. DRAKE. This is the 'Admiral Benbow,' a respectable house, and receives none but decent company; and I'll ask you to go somewhere else, for I don't like the looks of you.

PEW. Turn me away? Why, Lord love you, I'm David Pew—old David Pew—him as was Benbow's own particular cox'n. You wouldn't turn away old Pew from the sign of his late commander's 'ed? Ah, my British female, you'd have used me different if you'd seen me in the fight! [There laid old Benbow, both his legs shot off, in a basket, and the blessed spy-glass at his eye to that same hour: a picter, ma'am, of naval daring: when a round shot come, and took and knocked a bucketful of shivers right into my poor daylights. 'Damme,' says the Admiral, 'is that old Pew, my old Pew?' he says.—'It's old Pew, sir,' says the first lootenant, 'worse luck,' he says.—'Then damme,' says Admiral Benbow, 'if that's how they serve a lion-'arted seaman, damme if I care to live,' he says; and, ma'am, he laid down his spy-glass.]

MRS. DRAKE. Blind man, I don't fancy you, and that's the truth; and I'll thank you to take yourself off.

PEW. Thirty years have I fought for country and king, and now in my blind old age I'm to be sent packing from a measly public-'ouse? Mark ye, ma'am, if I go, you take the consequences. Is this a inn? Or haint it? If it is a inn, then by act of parleyment, I'm free to sling my 'ammick. Don't you forget: this is a act of parleyment job, this is. You look out.

MRS. DRAKE. Why, what's to do with the man and his acts of parliament? I don't want to fly in the face of an act of parliament, not I. If what you say is true—

PEW. True? If there's anything truer than a act of parleyment—Ah! you ask the beak. True? I've that in my 'art as makes me wish it wasn't.

MRS. DRAKE. I don't like to risk it. I don't like your looks, and you're more sea-lawyer than seaman to my mind. But I'll tell you what: if you can pay, you can stay. So there.

PEW. No chink, no drink? That's your motto, is it? Well, that's sense. Now, look here, ma'am, I ain't beautiful like you; but I'm good, and I'll give you warrant for it. Get me a noggin of rum, and suthin' to scoff, and a penny pipe, and a half-a-foot of baccy; and there's a guinea for the reckoning. There's plenty more in the locker; so bear a hand, and be smart. I don't like waiting; it ain't my way. (Exit MRS. DRAKE, R. PEW sits at the table, R. The settle conceals him from all the upper part of the stage.)

MRS. DRAKE (re-entering). Here's the rum, sailor.

PEW (drinks). Ah, rum! That's my sheet-anchor: rum and the blessed Gospel. Don't you forget that, ma'am: rum and the Gospel is old Pew's sheet-anchor. You can take for another while you're about it; and, I say, short reckonings make long friends, hey? Where's my change?

MRS. DRAKE. I'm counting it now. There, there it is, and thank you for your custom. (She goes out, R.)

PEW (calling after her). Don't thank me, ma'am; thank the act of parleyment! Rum, fourpence; two penny pieces and a Willi'm-and-Mary tizzy makes a shilling; and a spade half-guinea is eleven and six (re-enter MRS. DRAKE with supper, pipe, etc.); and a blessed majesty George the First crown-piece makes sixteen and six; and two shilling bits is eighteen and six; and a new half-crown makes—no it don't! O, no! Old Pew's too smart a hand to be bammed with a soft half-tusheroon.

MRS. DRAKE (changing piece). I'm sure I didn't know it, sailor.

PEW (trying new coin between his teeth). In course you didn't, my dear; but I did, and I thought I'd mention it. Is that my supper, hey? Do my nose deceive me? (Sniffing and feeling.) Cold duck? sage and onions? a round of double Gloster? and that noggin o' rum? Why, I declare if I'd stayed and took pot-luck with my old commander, Cap'n John Gaunt, he couldn't have beat this little spread, as I've got by act of parleyment.

MRS. DRAKE (at knitting). Do you know the captain, sailor?

PEW. Know him? I was that man's bos'un, ma'am. In the Guinea trade, we was known as 'Pew's Cap'n,' and 'Gaunt's Bo'sun,' one for other like. We was like two brothers, ma'am. And a excellent cold duck, to be sure; and the rum lovely.

MRS. DRAKE. If you know John Gaunt, you know his daughter Arethusa.

PEW. What? Arethusa? Know her, says you? know her? Why, Lord love you, I was her god-father. ['Pew,' says Jack Gaunt to me, 'Pew,' he says, 'you're a man,' he says; 'I like a man to be a man,' says he, 'and damme,' he says, 'I like you; and sink me,' says he, 'if you don't promise and vow in the name of that new-born babe,' he says, 'why damme, Pew,' says he, 'you're not the man I take you for.'] Yes, ma'am, I named that female; with my own 'ands I did; Arethusa, I named her; that was the name I give her; so now you know if I speak true. And if you'll be as good as get me another noggin of rum, why, we'll drink her 'elth with three times three. (Exit MRS. DRAKE: PEW eating. MRS. DRAKE re-entering with rum.)

[MRS. DRAKE. If what you say be true, sailor (and I don't say it isn't, mind!), it's strange that Arethusa and that godly man her father have never so much as spoke your name.

PEW. Why, that's so! And why, says you? Why, when I dropped in and paid my respecks this morning, do you think she knew me? No more'n a babe unborn! Why, ma'am, when I promised and vowed for her, I was the picter of a man-o'-war's man, I was: eye like a eagle; walked the deck in a hornpipe, foot up and foot down; v'ice as mellow as rum; 'and upon 'art, and all the females took dead aback at the first sight, Lord bless 'em! Know me? Not likely. And as for me, when I found her such a lovely woman—by the feel of her 'and and arm!—you might have knocked me down with a feather. But here's where it is, you see: when you've been knocking about on blue water for a matter of two-and-forty year, shipwrecked here, and blown up there, and everywhere out of luck, and given over for dead by all your messmates and relations, why, what it amounts to is this: nobody knows you, and you hardly know yourself, and there you are; and I'll trouble you for another noggin of rum.

MRS. DRAKE. I think you've had enough.

PEW. I don't; so bear a hand. (Exit MRS. DRAKE; PEW empties the glass.) Rum, ah, rum, you're a lovely creature; they haven't never done you justice. (Proceeds to fill and light pipe; re-enter MRS. DRAKE with rum.)] And now, ma'am, since you're so genteel and amicable-like, what about my old commander? Is he, in a manner of speaking, on half pay? or is he living on his fortune, like a gentleman slaver ought?

MRS. DRAKE. Well, sailor, people talk, you know.

PEW. I know, ma'am; I'd have been rolling in my coach, if they'd have held their tongues.

MRS. DRAKE. And they do say that Captain Gaunt, for so pious a man, is little better than a miser.

PEW. Don't say it, ma'am; not to old Pew. Ah, how often have I up and strove with him! 'Cap'n, live it down,' says I. 'Ah, Pew,' says he, 'you're a better man than I am,' he says; 'but dammne,' he says, 'money,' he says, 'is like rum to me.' (Insinuating.) And what about a old sea-chest, hey? a old sea-chest, strapped with brass bands?

MRS. DRAKE. Why, that'll be the chest in his parlour, where he has it bolted to the wall, as I've seen with my own eyes; and so might you, if you had eyes to see with.

PEW. No, ma'am, that ain't good enough; you don't bam old Pew. You never was in that parlour in your life.

MRS. DRAKE. I never was? Well, I declare!

PEW. Well then, if you was, where's the chest? Beside the chimbley, hey? (Winking.) Beside the table with the 'oly Bible?

MRS. DRAKE. No, sailor, you don't get any information out of me.

PEW. What, ma'am? Not to old Pew? Why, my god-child showed it me herself, and I told her where she'd find my name—P, E, W, Pew—cut out on the starn of it; and sure enough she did. Why, ma'am, it was his old money-box when he was in the Guinea trade; and they do say he keeps the rhino in it still.

MRS. DRAKE. No, sailor, nothing out of me! And if you want to know, you can ask the Admiral himself! (She crosses, L.)

PEW. Hey? Old girl fly? Then I reckon I must have a mate, if it was the parish bull.

SCENE II

To these, KIT, a little drunk

KIT (looking in over half-door). Mrs. Drake! Mother! Where are you? Come and welcome the prodigal!

MRS. DRAKE (coming forward to meet him as he enters; PEW remains concealed by the settle, smoking, drinking, and listening). Lord bless us and save us, if it ain't my boy! Give us a kiss.

KIT. That I will, and twenty if you like, old girl. (Kisses her.)

MRS. DRAKE. O Kit, Kit, you've been at those other houses, where the stuff they give you, my dear, it is poison for a dog.

[KIT. Round with friends, mother: only round with friends.

MRS. DRAKE. Well, anyway, you'll take a glass just to settle it, from me. (She brings the bottle, and fills for him.) There, that's pure; that'll do you no harm.] But O, Kit, Kit, I thought you were done with all this Jack-a-shoring.

KIT. What cheer, mother? I'm only a sheet in the wind; and who's the worse for it but me?

MRS. DRAKE. Ah, and that dear young lady; and her waiting and keeping single these two years for the love of you!

KIT. She, mother? she's heart of oak, she's true as steel, and good as gold; and she has my ring on her finger, too. But where's the use? The Admiral won't look at me.

MRS. DRAKE. Why not? You're as good a man as him any day.

KIT. Am I? He says I'm a devil, and swears that none of his flesh and blood—that's what he said, mother!—should lie at my mercy. That's what cuts me. If it wasn't for the good stuff I've been taking aboard, and the jolly companions I've been seeing it out with, I'd just go and make a hole in the water, and be done with it, I would, by George!

MRS. DRAKE. That's like you men. Ah, we know you, we that keeps a public-house—we know you, good and bad: you go off on a frolic and forget; and you never think of the women that sit crying at home.

KIT. Crying? Arethusa cry? Why, dame, she's the bravest-hearted girl in all broad England! Here, fill the glass! I'll win her yet. I drink to her; here's to her bright eyes, and here's to the blessed feet she walks upon!

PEW (looking round the corner of the settle). Spoke like a gallant seaman, every inch. Shipmate, I'm a man as has suffered, and I'd like to shake your fist, and drink a can of flip with you.

KIT (coming down). Hullo, my hearty! who the devil are you? Who's this, mother?

MRS. DRAKE. Nay, I know nothing about him. (She goes out, R.)

PEW. Cap'n, I'm a brother seaman, and my name is Pew, old David Pew, as you may have heard of in your time, he having sailed along of 'Awke and glorious Benbow, and a right-'and man to both.

KIT. Benbow? Steady, mate! D'ye mean to say you went to sea before you were born?

PEW. See now! The sign of this here inn was running in my 'ed, I reckon. Benbow, says you? no, not likely! Anson, I mean; Anson and Sir Edward 'Awke: that's the pair: I was their right-'and man.

KIT. Well, mate, you may be all that, and more; but you're a rum un to look at, anyhow.

PEW. Right you are, and so I am. But what is looks? It's the 'art that does it: the 'art is the seaman's star; and here's old David Pew's, a matter of fifty years at sea, but tough and sound as the British Constitootion.

KIT. You're right there, Pew. Shake hands upon it. And you're a man they're down upon, just like myself, I see. We're a pair of plain, good-hearted, jolly tars; and all these 'longshore fellows cock a lip at us, by George. What cheer, mate?

ARETHUSA (without). Mrs. Drake! Mrs. Drake!

PEW. What, a female? hey? a female? Board her board her, mate! I'm dark. (He retires again behind, to table, R., behind settle.)

ARETHUSA (without). Mrs. Drake!

MRS. DRAKE (re-entering and running to door). Here I am, my dear; come in.

SCENE III

To these, ARETHUSA

ARETHUSA. Ah, Kit, I've found you. I thought you would lodge with Mrs. Drake.

KIT. What? are you looking for your consort? Whistle, I'm your dog; I'll come to you. I've been toasting you fathom deep, my beauty; and with every glass I love you dearer.

ARETHUSA. Now Kit, if you want to please my father, this is not the way. Perhaps he thinks too much of the guineas: well, gather them—if you think me worth the price. Go you to your sloop, clinker built, eighty tons burthen—you see I remember, Skipper Kit! I don't deny I like a man of spirit; but if you care to please Captain Gaunt, keep out of taverns; and if you could carry yourself a bit more—more elderly!

[KIT. Can I? Would I? Ah, just couldn't and just won't I, then!

MRS. DRAKE. I hope, madam, you don't refer to my house; a publican I may be, but tavern is a word that I don't hold with; and here there's no bad drink, and no loose company; and as for my blessedest Kit, I declare I love him like my own.

ARETHUSA. Why, who could help it, Mrs. Drake?]

KIT. Arethusa, you're an angel. Do I want to please Captain Gaunt? Why, that's as much as ask whether I love you. [I don't deny that his words cut me; for they did. But as for wanting to please him, if he was deep as the blue Atlantic, I would beat it out. And elderly, too? Aha, you witch, you're wise! Elderly? You've set the course; you leave me alone to steer it. Matrimony's my port, and love is my cargo.] That's a likely question, ain't it, Mrs. Drake? Do I want to please him! Elderly, says you? Why, see here: Fill up my glass, and I'll drink to Arethusa on my knees.

ARETHUSA. Why, you stupid boy, do you think that would please him?

KIT. On my knees I'll drink it! (As he kneels and drains the glass, GAUNT enters, and he scrambles to his feet.)

SCENE IV

To these, GAUNT

GAUNT. Arethusa, this is no place for you.

ARETHUSA. No, father.

GAUNT. I wish you had been spared this sight; but look at him, child, since you are here; look at God's image, so debased. And you, young man (to KIT), you have proved that I was right. Are you the husband for this innocent maid?

KIT. Captain Gaunt, I have a word to say to you. Terror is your last word; you're bitter hard upon poor sinners, bitter hard and black—you that were a sinner yourself. These are not the true colours: don't deceive yourself; you're out of your course.

[GAUNT. Heaven forbid that I should be hard, Christopher. It is not I; it's God's law that is of iron. Think! if the blow were to fall now, some cord to snap within you, some enemy to plunge a knife into your heart; this room, with its poor taper light, to vanish; this world to disappear like a drowning man into the great ocean; and you, your brain still whirling, to be snatched into the presence of the eternal Judge: Christopher French, what answer would you make? For these gifts wasted, for this rich mercy scorned, for these high-handed bravings of your better angel,—what have you to say?

KIT. Well, sir, I want my word with you, and by your leave I'll have it out.

ARETHUSA. Kit, for pity's sake!

KIT. Arethusa, I don't speak to you, my dear: you've got my ring, and I know what that means. The man I speak to is Captain Gaunt. I came to-day as happy a man as ever stepped, and with as fair a look-out. What did you care? what was your reply? None of your flesh and blood, you said, should lie at the mercy of a wretch like me! Am I not flesh and blood that you should trample on me like that? Is that charity, to stamp the hope out of a poor soul?]

GAUNT. You speak wildly; or the devil of drink that is in you speaks instead.

KIT. You think me drunk? well, so I am, and whose fault is it but yours? It was I that drank; but you take your share of it, Captain Gaunt: you it was that filled the can.

GAUNT. Christopher French, I spoke but for your good, your good and hers. 'Woe unto him'—these are the dreadful words—'by whom offences shall come: it were better—' Christopher, I can but pray for both of us.

KIT. Prayers? Now I tell you freely, Captain Gaunt, I don't value your prayers. Deeds are what I ask; kind deeds and words—that's the true-blue piety: to hope the best and do the best, and speak the kindest. As for you, you insult me to my face; and then you'll pray for me? What's that? Insult behind my back is what I call it! No, sir; you're out of the course; you're no good man to my view, be you who you may.

MRS. DRAKE. O Christopher! To Captain Gaunt?

ARETHUSA. Father, father, come away!

KIT. Ah, you see? She suffers too; we all suffer. You spoke just now of a devil; well, I'll tell you the devil you have: the devil of judging others. And as for me, I'll get as drunk as Bacchus.

GAUNT. Come!

SCENE V

PEW, MRS. DRAKE, KIT

PEW (coming out and waving his pipe). Commander, shake! Hooray for old England! If there's anything in the world that goes to old Pew's 'art, it's argyment. Commander, you handled him like a babby, kept the weather gauge, and hulled him every shot. Commander, give it a name, and let that name be rum!

KIT. Ay, rum's the sailor's fancy. Mrs. Drake, a bottle and clean glasses.

MRS. DRAKE. Kit French, I wouldn't. Think better of it, there's a dear! And that sweet girl just gone!

PEW. Ma'am, I'm not a 'ard man; I'm not the man to up and force a act of parleyment upon a helpless female. But you see here: Pew's friends is sacred. Here's my friend here, a perfeck seaman, and a man with a 'ed upon his shoulders, and a man that, damme, I admire. He give you a order, ma'am:—march!

MRS. DRAKE. Kit, don't you listen to that blind man; he's the devil wrote upon his face.

PEW. Don't you insinuate against my friend. He ain't a child, I hope? he knows his business? Don't you get trying to go a lowering of my friend in his own esteem.

MRS. DRAKE. Well, I'll bring it, Kit; but it's against the grain. (Exit.)

KIT. I say, old boy, come to think of it, why should we? It's been glasses round with me all day. I've got my cargo.

PEW. You? and you just argy'd the 'ed off of Admiral Guinea? O stash that! I stand treat, if it comes to that!

KIT. What! Do I meet with a blind seaman and not stand him? That's not the man I am!

MRS. DRAKE (re-entering with bottle and glasses). There!

PEW. Easy does it, ma'am.

KIT. Mrs. Drake, you had better trot.

MRS. DRAKE. Yes, I'll trot; and I trot with a sick heart, Kit French, to leave you drinking your wits away with that low blind man. For a low man you are—a low blind man—and your clothes they would disgrace a scarecrow. I'll go to my bed, Kit; and O, dear boy, go soon to yours—the old room, you know; it's ready for you—and go soon and sleep it off; for you know, dear, they, one and all, regret it in the morning; thirty years I've kept this house, and one and all they did regret it, dear.

PEW. Come now, you walk!

MRS. DRAKE. O, it's not for your bidding. You a seaman? The ship for you to sail in is the hangman's cart.—Good-night, Kit dear, and better company!

SCENE VI

PEW, KIT. They sit at the other table, L.

PEW. Commander, here's her 'ealth!

KIT. Ay, that's the line: her health! But that old woman there is a good old woman, Pew.

PEW. So she is, Commander. But there's no woman understands a seaman; now you and me, being both bred to it, we splice by natur'. As for A. G., if argyment can win her, why, she's yours. If I'd a-had your 'ed for argyment, damme, I'd a-been a Admiral, I would! And if argyment won't win her, well, see here, you put your trust in David Pew.

KIT. David Pew, I don't know who you are, David Pew; I never heard of you; I don't seem able to clearly see you. Mrs. Drake, she's a smart old woman, Pew, and she says you've the devil in your face.

PEW. Ah, and why, says you? Because I up and put her in her place, when she forgot herself to you, Commander.

KIT. Well, Pew, that's so; you stood by me like a man. Shake hands, Pew; and we'll make a night of it, or we'll know why, old boy!

PEW. That's my way. That's Pew's way, that is. That's Pew's way all over. Commander, excuse the liberty; but when I was your age, making allowance for a lowlier station and less 'ed for argyment, I was as like you as two peas. I know it by the v'ice (sings)—

'We hadn't been three days at sea before we saw a sail,   So we clapped on every stitch would stand, although it blew a gale,   And we walked along full fourteen knots, for the barkie she did know   As well as ever a soul on board, 'twas time for us to go.'

Chorus, Cap'n!

PEW and KIT (in chorus)—

'Time for us to go,
Time for us to go,
As well as ever a soul on board,
'Twas time for us to go.'

PEW (sings)—

'We carried away the royal yard, and the stunsail boom was gone;   Says the skipper, "They may go or stand, I'm damned if I don't crack   on;"   So the weather braces we'll round in, and the trysail set also,   And we'll keep the brig three p'ints away, for it's time for us to   go.

Give it mouth, Commander!

PEW and KIT (in chorus)—

'Time for us to go,
Time for us to go,
And we'll keep the brig three p'ints away,
For it's time for us to go.'

PEW. I ain't sung like that since I sang to Admiral 'Awke, the night before I lost my eyes, I ain't. 'Sink me!' says he, says Admiral 'Awke, my old commander (touching his hat), 'sink me!' he says, 'if that ain't 'art-of-oak,' he says: "art-of-oak,' says he, 'and a pipe like a bloody blackbird!' Commander, here's my respecks, and the devil fly away with Admiral Guinea!

KIT. I say, Pew, how's this? How do you know about Admiral Guinea? I say, Pew, I begin to think you know too much.

PEW. I ax your pardon; but as a man with a 'ed for argyment—and that's your best p'int o' sailing, Commander; intelleck is your best p'int—as a man with a 'ed for argyment, how do I make it out?

KIT. Aha, you're a sly dog, you're a deep dog, Pew; but you can't get the weather of Kit French. How do I make it out? I'll tell you. I make it out like this: Your name's Pew, ain't it? Very well. And you know Admiral Guinea, and that's his name, eh? Very well. Then you're Pew; and the Admiral's the Admiral; and you know the Admiral; and by George, that's all. Hey? Drink about, boys, drink about!

PEW. Lord love you, if I'd a-had a 'ed like yours! Why the Admiral was my first cap'n. I was that man's bo'sun, I was, aboard the Arethusa; and we was like two brothers. Did you never hear of Guinea-land and the black ivory business? (sings)—

'A quick run to the south we had, and when we made the Bight   We kept the offing all day long and crossed the bar at night.   Six hundred niggers in the hold and seventy we did stow,   And when we'd clapped the hatches on, 'twas time for us to go.'

Lay forward, lads!

KIT and PEW (in chorus)—

'Time for us to go,' etc.

KIT. I say, Pew, I like you; you're a damned ugly dog; but I like you. But look ye here, Pew: fair does it, you know, or we part company this minute. If you and the Ad—the Admirable were like brothers on the Guinea coast, why aren't you like brothers here?

PEW. Ah, I see you coming. What a 'ed! what a 'ed! Since Pew is a friend of the family, says you, why didn't he sail in and bear a hand, says you, when you was knocking the Admiral's ship about his ears in argyment?

KIT. Well, Pew, now you put a name to it, why not?

PEW. Ah, why not? There I recko'nise you. [Well, see here: argyment's my weakness, in a manner of speaking; I wouldn't a-borne down and spiled sport, not for gold untold, no, not for rum, I wouldn't! And besides, Commander, I put it to you, as between man and man, would it have been seaman-like to let on and show myself to a old shipmate, when he was yard-arm to yard-arm with a craft not half his metal, and getting blown out of water every broadside? Would it have been 'ansome? I put it to you, as between man and man.

KIT. Pew, I may have gifts; but I never thought of that. Why, no: not seaman-like. Pew, you've a heart; that's what I like you for.

PEW. Ah, that I have: you'll see. I wanted—now you follow me—I wanted to keep square with Admiral Guinea.] Why? says you. Well, put it that I know a fine young fellow when I sees him; and put it that I wish him well; and put it, for the sake of argyment, that the father of that lovely female's in my power. Aha? Pew's Power! Why, in my 'ands he's like this pocket 'andke'cher. Now, brave boy, do you see?

KIT. No, Pew, my head's gone; I don't see.

PEW. Why, cheer up, Commander! You want to marry this lovely female?

KIT. Ay, that I do; but I'm not fit for her, Pew; I'm a drunken dog, and I'm not fit for her.

PEW. Now, Cap'n, you'll allow a old seaman to be judge: one as sailed with 'Awke and blessed Benb— with 'Awke and noble Anson. You've been open and above-board with me, and I'll do the same by you: it being the case that you're hard hit about a lovely woman, which many a time and oft it has happened to old Pew; and him with a feeling 'art that bleeds for you, Commander; why look here: I'm that girl's godfather; promised and vowed for her, I did; and I like you; and you're the man for her; and, by the living Jacob, you shall splice!

KIT. David Pew, do you mean what you say?

PEW. Do I mean what I say? Does David Pew? Ask Admiral 'Awke! Ask old Admiral Byng in his coffin, where I laid him with these lands! Pew does, is what those naval commanders would reply. Mean it? I reckon so.

KIT. Then, shake hands. You're an honest man, Pew—old Pew!—and I'll make your fortune. But there's something else, if I could keep the run of it. O, ah! But can you? That's the point. Can you; don't you see?

PEW. Can I? You leave that to me; I'll bring you to your moorings; I'm the man that can, and I'm him that will. But only, look here, let's understand each other. You're a bold blade, ain't you? You won't stick at a trifle for a lovely female? You'll back me up? You're a man, ain't you? a man, and you'll see me through and through it, hey? Come; is that so? Are you fair and square and stick at nothing?

KIT. Me, Pew? I'll go through fire and water.

PEW. I'll risk it.—Well, then, see here, my son: another swallow and we jog.

KIT. No, not to-night, Pew, not to-night!

PEW. Commander, in a manner of speaking, wherefore?

KIT. Wherefore, Pew? 'Cause why, Pew? 'Cause I'm drunk, and be damned to you!

PEW. Commander, I ax your pardon; but, saving your presence, that's a lie. What? drunk? a man with a 'ed for argyment like that? just you get up, and steady yourself on your two pins, and you'll be as right as ninepence.

[KIT. Pew, before we budge, let me shake your flipper again. You're heart of oak, Pew, sure enough; and if you can bring the Adam—Admirable about, why, damme, I'll make your fortune! How you're going to do it, I don't know; but I'll stand by; and I know you'll do it if anybody can. But I'm drunk, Pew; you can't deny that: I'm as drunk as a Plymouth fiddler, Pew; and how you're going to do it is a mystery to me.

PEW. Ah, you leave that to me. All I want is what I've got: your promise to stand by and bear a hand (producing a dark lantern).] Now, here, you see, is my little glim; it ain't for me, because I'm blind, worse luck! and the day and night is the blessed same to David Pew. But you watch. You put the candle near me. Here's what there ain't many blind men could do, take the pick o' them! (lighting a screw of paper, and with that, the lantern). Hey? That's it. Hey? Go and pity the poor blind!

KIT (while PEW blows out the candles). But I say, Pew, what do you want with it?

PEW. To see by, my son. (He shuts the lantern and puts it in his pocket. Stage quite dark. Moonlight at window.) All ship-shape? No sparks about? No? Come, then, lean on me and heave ahead for the lovely female. (Singing sotto voce)

'Time for us to go,
Time for us to go,
And when we'd clapped the hatches on,
'Twas time for us to go.'

ACT - CURTAIN DROP.

ACT III.

The Stage represents the Admiral's house, as in Act I. GAUNT seated, is reading aloud; ARETHUSA sits at his feet. Candles

SCENE I

ARETHUSA, GAUNT

[GAUNT (reading). 'And Ruth said, Intreat me not to leave thee, or to return from following after thee: for whither thou goest, I will go; and where thou lodgest, I will lodge: thy people shall be my people, and thy God my God: Where thou diest, will I die, and there will I be buried: the Lord do so to me, and more also, if aught but death part thee and me.' (He closes the book.) Amen.

ARETHUSA. Amen. Father, there spoke my heart.]

GAUNT. Arethusa, the Lord in his mercy has seen right to vex us with trials of many kinds. It is a little matter to endure the pangs of the flesh: the smart of wounds, the passion of hunger and thirst, the heaviness of disease; and in this world I have learned to take thought for nothing save the quiet of your soul. It is through our affections that we are smitten with the true pain, even the pain that kills.

ARETHUSA. And yet this pain is our natural lot. Father, I fear to boast, but I know that I can bear it. Let my life, then, flow like common lives, each pain rewarded with some pleasure, each pleasure linked with some pain: nothing pure whether for good or evil: and my husband, like myself and all the rest of us, only a poor, kind-hearted sinner, striving for the better part. What more could any woman ask?

GAUNT. Child, child, your words are like a sword. What would she ask? Look upon me whom, in the earthly sense, you are commanded to respect. Look upon me: do I bear a mark? is there any outward sign to bid a woman avoid and flee from me?

ARETHUSA. I see nothing but the face I love.

GAUNT. There is none: nor yet on the young man Christopher, whose words still haunt and upbraid me. Yes, I am hard; I was born hard, born a tyrant, born to be what I was, a slaver captain. But to-night, and to save you, I will pluck my heart out of my bosom. You shall know what makes me what I am; you shall hear, out of my own life, why I dread and deprecate this marriage. Child, do you remember your mother?

ARETHUSA. Remember her? Ah, if she had been here to-day!

GAUNT. It is thirteen years since she departed, and took with her the whole sunshine of my life. Do you remember the manner of her departure? You were a child, and cannot; but I can and do. Remember? shall I ever forget? Here or hereafter, ever forget! Ten years she was my wife, and ten years she lay a-dying. Arethusa, she was a saint on earth; and it was I that killed her.

ARETHUSA. Killed her? my mother? You?

GAUNT. Not with my hand; for I loved her. I would not have hurt one hair upon her head. But she got her death by me, as sure as by a blow.

ARETHUSA. I understand—I can see: you brood on trifles, misunderstandings, unkindnesses you think them; though my mother never knew of them, or never gave them a second thought. It is natural, when death has come between.

GAUNT. I married her from Falmouth. She was comely as the roe; I see her still—her dove's eyes and her smile! I was older than she; and I had a name for hardness, a hard and wicked man; but she loved me—my Hester!—and she took me as I was. O how I repaid her trust! Well, our child was born to us; and we named her after the brig I had built and sailed, the old craft whose likeness—older than you, girl—stands there above our heads. And so far, that was happiness. But she yearned for my salvation; and it was there I thwarted her. My sins were a burden upon her spirit, a shame to her in this world, her terror in the world to come. She talked much and often of my leaving the devil's trade I sailed in. She had a tender and a Christian heart, and she would weep and pray for the poor heathen creatures that I bought and sold and shipped into misery, till my conscience grew hot within me. I've put on my hat, and gone out and made oath that my next cargo should be my last; but it never was, that oath was never kept. So I sailed again and again for the Guinea coast, until the trip came that was to be my last indeed. Well, it fell out that we had good luck trading, and I stowed the brig with these poor heathen as full as she would hold. We had a fair run westward till we were past the line, but one night the wind rose and there came a hurricane, and for seven days we were tossed on the deep seas, in the hardest straits, and every hand on deck. For several days they were battened down: all that time we heard their cries and lamentations, but worst at the beginning; and when at last, and near dead myself, I crept below—O! some they were starved, some smothered, some dead of broken limbs; and the hold was like a lazar-house in the time of the anger of the Lord!

ARETHUSA. O!

GAUNT. It was two hundred and five that we threw overboard: two hundred and five lost souls that I had hurried to their doom. I had many die with me before; but not like that—not such a massacre as that; and I stood dumb before the sight. For I saw I was their murderer—body and soul their murderer; and, Arethusa, my Hester knew it. That was her death-stroke: it felled her. She had long been dying slowly; but from the hour she heard that story, the garment of the flesh began to waste and perish, the fountains of her life dried up; she faded before my face; and in two months from my landing—O Hester, Hester, would God I had died for thee!

ARETHUSA. Mother! O poor soul! O poor father! O father, it was hard on you.

GAUNT. The night she died, she lay there, in her bed. She took my hand. 'I am going,' she said, 'to heaven. For Christ's sake,' she said, 'come after me, and bring my little maid. I'll be waiting and wearying till you come;' and she kissed my hand, the hand that killed her. At that I broke out calling on her to stop, for it was more than I could bear. But no, she said she must still tell me of my sins, and how the thought of them had bowed down her life. 'And O!' she said, 'if I couldn't prevail on you alive, let my death.' . . . Well, then, she died. What have I done since then? I've laid my course for Hester. Sin, temptation, pleasure, all this poor shadow of a world, I saw them not: I saw my Hester waiting, waiting and wearying. I have made my election sure; my sins I have cast them out. Hester, Hester, I will come to you, poor waiting one; and I'll bring your little maid: ay, dearest soul, I'll bring your little maid safe with me!

ARETHUSA. O teach me how! Show me the way! only show me.—O mother, mother!—If it were paved with fire, show me the way, and I will walk it bare-foot!

GAUNT. They call me a miser. They say that in this sea-chest of mine I hoard my gold. (He passes R. to chest, takes out key, and unlocks it.) They think my treasure and my very soul are locked up here. They speak after the flesh, but they are right. See!

ARETHUSA. Her watch? the wedding ring? O father, forgive me!

GAUNT. Ay, her watch that counted the hours when I was away; they were few and sorrowful, my Hester's hours; and this poor contrivance numbered them. The ring—with that I married her. This chain, it's of Guinea gold; I brought it home for her, the year before we married, and she wore it to her wedding. It was a vanity: they are all vanities; but they are the treasure of my soul. Below here, see, her wedding dress. Ay, the watch has stopped: dead, dead. And I know that my Hester died of me; and day and night, asleep and awake, my soul abides in her remembrance.

ARETHUSA. And you come in your sleep to look at them. O poor father! I understand—I understand you now.

GAUNT. In my sleep? Ay? do I so? My Hester!

ARETHUSA. And why, why did you not tell me? I thought—I was like the rest!—I feared you were a miser. O, you should have told me; I should have been so proud—so proud and happy. I knew you loved her; but not this, not this.

GAUNT. Why should I have spoken? It was all between my Hester and me.

ARETHUSA. Father, may I speak? May I tell you what my heart tells me? You do not understand about my mother. You loved her—O, as few men can love. And she loved you: think how she loved you! In this world, you know—you have told me—there is nothing perfect. All we men and women have our sins; and they are a pain to those that love us, and the deeper the love, the crueller the pain. That is life; and it is life we ask, not heaven; and what matter for the pain, if only the love holds on? Her love held: then she was happy! Her love was immortal; and when she died, her one grief was to be parted from you, her one hope to welcome you again.

GAUNT. And you, Arethusa: I was to bring her little maid.

ARETHUSA. God bless her, yes, and me! But, father, can you not see that she was blessed among women?

GAUNT. Child, child, you speak in ignorance; you touch upon griefs you cannot fathom.

ARETHUSA. No, dearest, no. She loved you, loved you and died of it. Why else do women live? What would I ask but just to love my Kit and die for him, and look down from heaven, and see him keep my memory holy and live the nobler for my sake?

GAUNT. Ay, do you so love him?

ARETHUSA. Even as my mother loved my father.

GAUNT. Ay? Then we will see. What right have I—You are your mother's child: better, tenderer, wiser than I. Let us seek guidance in prayer. Good-night, my little maid.

ARETHUSA. O father, I know you at last.

SCENE II

GAUNT and ARETHUSA go out, L., carrying the candles. Stage dark. A distant clock chimes the quarters, and strikes one. Then, the tap-tapping of Pew's stick is hear without; the key is put into the lock; and enter PEW, C., he pockets key, and is followed by KIT, with dark lantern

PEW. Quiet, you lubber! Can't you foot it soft, you that has daylights and a glim?

KIT. All right, old boy. How the devil did we get through the door? Shall I knock him up?

PEW. Stow your gab (seizing his wrist). Under your breath!

KIT. Avast that! You're a savage dog, aren't you?

PEW. Turn on that glim.

KIT. It's as light as a trivet, Pew. What next? By George, Pew, I'll make your fortune.

PEW. Here, now, look round this room, and sharp. D'ye see a old sea-chest?

KIT. See it, Pew? why, d'ye think I'm blind?

PEW. Take me across, and let me feel of her. Mum; catch my hand. Ah, that's her (feeling the chest), that's the Golden Mary. Now, see here, my bo, if you've the pluck of a weevil in a biscuit, this girl is yours; if you hain't, and think to sheer off, I'm blind, but I'm deadly.

KIT. You'll keep a civil tongue in your head all the same. I'll take threats from nobody, blind or not. Let's knock up the Admiral and be done with it. What I want is to get rid of this dark lantern. It makes me feel like a housebreaker, by George.

PEW (seated on chest). You follow this. I'm sick of drinking bilge, when I might be rolling in my coach, and I'm dog-sick of Jack Gaunt. Who's he to be wallowing in gold, when a better man is groping crusts in the gutter and spunging for rum? Now, here in this blasted chest is the gold to make men of us for life: gold, ay, gobs of it; and writin's too—things that if I had the proof of 'em I'd hold Jack Gaunt to the grindstone till his face was flat. I'd have done it single-handed; but I'm blind, worse luck: I'm all in the damned dark here, poking with a stick—Lord, burn up with lime the eyes that saw it! That's why I raked up you. Come, out with your iron, and prise the lid off. You shall touch your snack, and have the wench for nothing; ay, and fling her in the street, when done.

KIT. So you brought me here to steal did you?

PEW. Ay did I; and you shall. I'm a biter: I bring blood.

KIT. Now, Pew, you came here on my promise, or I'd kill you like a rat. As it is, out of that door! One, two, three (drawing his cutlass), and off!

PEW (leaping at his throat, and with a great voice). Help! murder! thieves!

SCENE III

To these, ARETHUSA, GAUNT, with lights. Stage light. PEW has KIT down, and is throttling him

PEW. I've got him, Cap'n. What, kill my old commander, and rob him of his blessed child? Not with old Pew!

GAUNT. Get up, David: can't you see you're killing him? Unhand, I say.

ARETHUSA. In heaven's name, who is it?

PEW. It's a damned villain, my pretty; and his name, to the best of my belief, is French.

ARETHUSA. Kit? Kit French? Never!

KIT (rising). He's done for me. (Falls on chest.)

[PEW. Don't you take on about him, ducky; he ain't worth it. Cap'n Gaunt, I took him and I give him up. You was 'ard on me this morning, Cap'n: this is my way Pew's way, this is—of paying of you out.

ARETHUSA. Father, this is the blind man that came while you were abroad. Sure you'll not listen to him. And you, Kit, you, what is this?

KIT. Captain Gaunt, that blind devil has half-throttled me. He brought me here—I can't speak—he has almost killed me—and I'd been drinking too.

GAUNT. And you, David Pew, what do you say?]

PEW. Cap'n, the rights of it is this. Me and that young man there was partaking in a friendly drop of rum at the Admiral Benbow inn; and I'd just proposed his blessed Majesty, when the young man he ups and says to me: 'Pew,' he says, 'I like you, Pew: you're a true seaman,' he says; 'and I'm one as sticks at nothing; and damme, Pew,' he says, 'I'll make your fortune.' [Can he deny as them was his words? Look at him, you as has eyes: no, he cannot. 'Come along of me,' he says, 'and damme, I'll make your fortune.'] Well, Cap'n, he lights a dark lantern (which you'll find it somewhere on the floor, I reckon), and out we goes, me follerin' his lead, as I thought was 'art-of-oak and a true-blue mariner; and the next I knows is, here we was in here, and him a-askin' me to 'old the glim, while he prised the lid off of your old sea-chest with his cutlass.

GAUNT. The chest? (He leaps, R., and examines chest.) Ah!

PEW. Leastways, I was to 'elp him, by his account of it, while he nailed the rhino, and then took and carried off that lovely maid of yours; for a lovely maid she is, and one as touched old Pew's 'art Cap'n, when I 'eard that, my blood biled. 'Young man,' I says, 'you don't know David Pew,' I says; and with that I ups and does my dooty by him, cutlass and all, like a lion-'arted seaman, though blind. [And then in comes you, and I gives him up: as you know for a fack is true, and I'll subscribe at the Assizes. And that, if you was to cut me into junks, is the truth, the 'ole truth, and nothing but the truth, world without end, so help me, amen; and if you'll 'and me over the 'oly Bible, me not having such a thing about me at the moment, why, I'll put a oath upon it like a man.]

ARETHUSA. Father, have you heard?

[GAUNT. I know this man, Arethusa, and the truth is not in him.

ARETHUSA. Well, and why do we wait? We know Kit, do we not?

KIT. Ay, Captain, you know the pair of us, and you can see his face and mine.]

GAUNT. Christopher, the facts are all against you. I find you here in my house at midnight: you who at least had eyes to see, and must have known whither you were going. It was this man, not you, who called me up: and when I came in, it was he who was uppermost and who gave you up to justice. This unsheathed cutlass is yours; there hangs the scabbard, empty; and as for the dark lantern, of what use is light to the blind? and who could have trimmed and lighted it but you?

PEW. Ah, Cap'n, what a 'ed for argyment!

KIT. And now, sir, now that you have spoken, I claim the liberty to speak on my side.

GAUNT. Not so. I will first have done with this man, David Pew, it were too simple to believe your story as you tell it; but I can find no testimony against you. From whatever reason, assuredly you have done me service. Here are five guineas to set you on your way. Begone at once; and while it is yet time, think upon your repentance.

PEW. Cap'n, here's my respecks. You've turned a pious man, Cap'n; it does my 'art good to 'ear you. But you ain't the only one. O no! I came about and paid off on the other tack before you, I reckon: you ask the Chaplain of the Fleet else, as called me on the quarter-deck before old Admiral 'Awke himself (touching his hat), my old commander. ['David Pew,' he says, 'five-and-thirty year have I been in this trade, man and boy,' that chaplain says, 'and damme, Pew,' says he, 'if ever I seen the seaman that could rattle off his catechism within fifty mile of you. Here's five guineas out of my own pocket,' he says; 'and what's more to the pint,' he says, 'I'll speak to my reverend brother-in-law, the Bishop of Dover,' he says; 'and if ever you leave the sea, and wants a place as beadle, why damme,' says he, 'you go to him, for you're the man for him, and him for you.'

GAUNT. David Pew, you never set your foot on a King's ship in all your life. There lies the road.

PEW. Ah, you was always a 'ard man, Cap'n, and a 'ard man to believe, like Didymus the 'Ebrew prophet. But it's time for me to go, and I'll be going. My service to you, Cap'n: and I kiss my 'and to that lovely female.

'Time for us to go,
Time for us to go,
And when we'd clapped the hatches on,
'Twas time for us to go.'

SCENE IV

KIT, ARETHUSA, GAUNT

ARETHUSA. Now, Kit?

KIT. Well, sir, and now?

GAUNT. I find you here in my house at this untimely and unseemly hour; I find you there in company with one who, to my assured knowledge, should long since have swung in the wind at Execution Dock. What brought you? Why did you open my door while I slept to such a companion? Christopher French, I have two treasures. One (laying his hand on ARETHUSA'S shoulder) I know you covet. Christopher, is this your love?

KIT. Sir, I have been fooled and trapped. That man declared he knew you, declared he could make you change your mind about our marriage. I was drunk, sir, and I believed him: heaven knows I am sober now, and can see my folly; but I believed him then, and followed him. He brought me here, he told me your chest was full of gold that would make men of us for life. At that I saw my fault, sir, and drew my cutlass; and he, in the wink of an eye, roared out for help, leaped at my throat like a weasel and had me rolling on the floor. He was quick, and I, as I tell you, sir, was off my balance.

GAUNT. Is this man, Pew, your enemy?

KIT. No sir; I never saw him till to-night.

GAUNT. Then, if you must stand the justice of your country, come to the proof with a better plea. What? lantern and cutlass yours; you the one that knew the house; you the one that saw; you the one overtaken and denounced; and you spin me a galley yarn like that? If that is all your defence, you'll hang, sir, hang.

ARETHUSA. Ah! Father, I give him up: I will never see him, never speak to him, never think of him again; I take him from my heart; I give myself wholly up to you and to my mother; I will obey you in every point—O, not at a word merely—at a finger raised! I will do all this; I will do anything—anything you bid me; I swear it in the face of heaven. Only—Kit! I love him, father, I love him. Let him go.

[GAUNT. Go?

ARETHUSA. You let the other. Open the door again—for my sake, father—in my mother's name—O, open the door and let him go.]

KIT. Let me go? My girl, if you had cast me out is morning, good and well: I would have left you, though it broke my heart. But it's a changed story now; now I'm down on my luck, and you come and stab me from behind. I ask no favour, and I'll take none; I stand here on my innocence, and God helping me I'll clear my good name, and get your love again, if it's love worth having. [Now, Captain Gaunt, I've said my say, and you may do your pleasure. I am my father's son, and I never feared to face the truth.

GAUNT. You have spoken like a man, French, and you may go. I leave you free.

KIT. Nay, sir, not so: not with my will. I'm accused and counted guilty; the proofs are against me; the girl I love has turned upon me. I'll accept no mercy at your hands.] Captain Gaunt, I am your prisoner.

ARETHUSA. Kit, dear Kit—

GAUNT. Silence! Young man, I have offered you liberty without bond or condition. You refuse. You shall be judged. Meanwhile (opening the door, R.), you will go in here. I keep your cutlass. The night brings counsel: to-morrow shall decide. (He locks KIT in, leaving the key in the door.)

SCENE V

GAUNT, ARETHUSA, afterwards PEW

ARETHUSA. Father, you believe in him; you do; I know you do.

GAUNT. Child, I am not given to be hasty. I will pray and sleep upon this matter. (A knocking at the door, C.) Who knocks so late? (He opens.)

PEW (entering). Cap'n, shall I fetch the constable?

GAUNT. No.

PEW. No? Have ye killed him?

GAUNT. My man, I'll see you into the road. (He takes PEW by the arm, and goes out with him.)

SCENE VI

ARETHUSA

ARETHUSA. (Listens; then running to door, R.) Kit—dearest! wait! I will come to you soon. (GAUNT re-enters, C., as the drop falls.)

ACT - CURTAIN DROP.

ACT IV.

The Stage represents the Admiral's house, as in Acts I. and III. A chair, L., in front. As the curtain rises, the Stage is dark. Enter ARETHUSA, L., with candle; she lights another; and passes to door, R., which she unbolts. Stage light

SCENE I

ARETHUSA, KIT

ARETHUSA. Come, dear Kit, come!

KIT. Well, I'm here.

ARETHUSA. O Kit, you are not angry with me.

KIT. Have I reason to be pleased?

ARETHUSA. Kit, I was wrong. Forgive me.

KIT. O yes. I forgive you. I suppose you meant it kindly; but there are some kindnesses a man would rather die than take a gift of. When a man is accused, Arethusa, it is not that he fears the gallows—it's the shame that cuts him. At such a time as that, the way to help was to stand to your belief. You should have nailed my colours to the mast, not spoke of striking them. If I were to be hanged to-morrow, and your love there, and a free pardon and a dukedom on the other side—which would I choose?

ARETHUSA. Kit, you must judge me fairly. It was not my life that was at stake, it was yours. Had it been mine—mine, Kit—what had you done, then?

KIT. I am a downright fool; I saw it inside out. Why, give you up, by George!

ARETHUSA. Ah, you see! Now you understand. It was all pure love. When he said that word—O!—death and that disgrace! . . . But I know my father. He fears nothing so much as the goodness of his heart; and yet it conquers. He would pray, he said: and to-night, and by the kindness of his voice, I knew he was convinced already. All that is wanted, is that you should forgive me.

KIT. Arethusa, if you looked at me like that I'd forgive you piracy on the high seas. I was only sulky; I was boxed up there in the black dark, and couldn't see my hand. It made me pity that blind man, by George!

ARETHUSA. O, that blind man! The fiend! He came back, Kit: did you hear him? he thought we had killed you—you!

KIT. Well, well, it serves me right for keeping company with such a swab.

ARETHUSA. One thing puzzles me: how did you get in? I saw my father lock the door.

KIT. Ah, how? That's just it. I was a sheet in the wind, you see. How did we? He did it somehow... . By George, he had a key! He can get in again.

ARETHUSA. Again? that man!

KIT. Ay, can he! Again! When he likes!

ARETHUSA. Kit, I am afraid. O Kit, he will kill my father.

KIT. Afraid. I'm glad of that. Now, you'll see I'm worth my salt at something. Ten to one he's back to Mrs. Drake's. I'll after, and lay him aboard.

ARETHUSA. O Kit, he is too strong for you.

KIT. Arethusa, that's below the belt! Never you fear; I'll give a good account of him.

ARETHUSA (taking cutlass from the wall). You'll be none the worse for this, dear.

KIT. That's so (making cuts). All the same, I'm half ashamed to draw on a blind man; it's too much odds. (He leaps suddenly against the table.) Ah!

ARETHUSA. Kit! Are you ill?

KIT. My head's like a humming top; it serves me right for drinking.

ARETHUSA. O, and the blind man! (She runs, L., to the corner cupboard, brings a bottle and glass, and fills and offers glass.) Here, lad, drink that.

KIT. To you! That's better. (Bottle and glass remain on Gaunt's table.)

ARETHUSA. Suppose you miss him?

KIT. Miss him! The road is straight; and I can hear the tap-tapping of that stick a mile away.

ARETHUSA (listening). St! my father stirring in his room!

KIT. Let me get clear; tell him why when I'm gone. The door—?

ARETHUSA. Locked!

KIT. The window!

ARETHUSA. Quick, quick! (She unfastens R. window, by which KIT goes out.)

SCENE II

ARETHUSA, GAUNT entering L.

ARETHUSA. Father, Kit is gone . . . He is asleep.

GAUNT. Waiting, waiting and wearying. The years, they go so heavily, my Hester still waiting! (He goes R. to chest, which he opens.) That is your chain; it's of Guinea gold; I brought it you from Guinea. (Taking out chain.) You liked it once; it pleased you long ago; O, why not now—why will you not be happy now? . . . I swear this is my last voyage; see, I lay my hand upon the Holy Book and swear it. One more venture—for the child's sake, Hester; you don't think upon your little maid.

ARETHUSA. Ah, for my sake, it was for my sake!

GAUNT. Ten days out from Lagos. That's a strange sunset, Mr. Yeo. All hands shorten sail! Lay aloft there, look smart! . . . What's that? Only the negroes in the hold . . . Mr. Yeo, she can't live long at this; I have a wife and child in Barnstaple. . . . Christ, what a sea! Hold on, for God's sake—hold on fore and aft! Great God! (as thought the sea were making a breach over the ship at the moment).

ARETHUSA. O!

GAUNT. They seem quieter down below there . . . No water—no light—no air—seven days battened down, and the seas mountain high, and the ship labouring hell-deep! Two hundred and five, two hundred and five, two hundred and five—all to eternal torture!

ARETHUSA. O pity him, pity him! Let him sleep, let him forget! Let her prayers avail in heaven, and let him rest!

GAUNT. Hester, no, don't smile at me. Rather tears! I have seen you weep—often, often; two hundred and five times. Two hundred and five! (With ring.) Hester, here is your ring (he tries to put the ring on his finger). How comes it in my hand? Not fallen off again? O no, impossible! it was made smaller, dear, it can't have fallen off! Ah, you waste away. You must live, you must, for the dear child's sake, for mine, Hester, for mine! Ah, the child. Yes. Who am I to judge? Poor Kit French! And she, your little maid, she's like you, Hester, and she will save him! How should a man be saved without a wife?

ARETHUSA. O father, if you could but hear me thank and bless you! (The tapping of Pew's stick is heard approaching. GAUNT passes L. front and sits.)

GAUNT (beginning to count the taps). One—two—two hundred and five

ARETHUSA (listening). God help me, the blind man! (She runs to door, C.; the key is put into the lock from without, and the door opens.)

SCENE III

ARETHUSA (at back of stage by the door); GAUNT (front L.); to these, PEW, C.

PEW (sotto voce). All snug. (Coming down.) So that was you, my young friend Christopher, as shot by me on the road; and so you was hot foot after old Pew? Christopher, my young friend, I reckon I'll have the bowels out of that chest, and I reckon you'll be lagged and scragged for it. (At these words ARETHUSA locks the door, and takes the key.) What's that? All still. There's something wrong about this room. Pew, my 'art of oak, you're queer to-night; brace up, and carry off. Where's the tool? (Producing knife.) Ah, here she is; and now for the chest; and the gold; and rum—rum—rum. What! Open? . . . old clothes, by God! . . . He's done me; he's been before me; he's bolted with the swag; that's why he ran: Lord wither and waste him forty year for it! O Christopher, if I had my fingers on your throat! Why didn't I strangle the soul out of him? I heard the breath squeak in his weasand; and Jack Gaunt pulled me off. Ah, Jack, that's another I owe you. My pious friend, if I was God Almighty for five minutes! (GAUNT rises and begins to pace the stage like a quarterdeck, L.) What's that? A man's walk. He don't see me, thank the blessed dark! But it's time to slip, my bo. (He gropes his way stealthily till he comes to Gaunt's table, where he burns his hand in the candle.) A candle—lighted—then it's bright as day! Lord God, doesn't he see me? It's the horrors come alive. (GAUNT draws near and turns away.) I'll go mad, mad! (He gropes to the door, stopping and starting.) Door. (His voice rising for the first time, sharp with terror.) Locked? Key gone? Trapped! Keep off—keep off of me—keep away! (Sotto voce again.) Keep your head, Lord have mercy, keep your head. I'm wet with sweat. What devil's den is this? I must out—out! (He shakes the door vehemently.) No? Knife it is then—knife—knife—knife! (He moves with the knife raised towards GAUNT, intently listening, and changing his direction as GAUNT changes his position on the stage.)

ARETHUSA (rushing to intercept him). Father, father, wake!

GAUNT. Hester, Hester! (He turns, in time to see ARETHUSA grapple PEW in the centre of the Stage, and PEW force her down.)

ARETHUSA. Kit! Kit!

PEW (with the knife raised). Pew's way!

SCENE IV

To these, KIT

(He leaps through window, R., and cuts PEW down. At the same moment, GAUNT, who has been staring helplessly at his daughter's peril, fully awakes.)

GAUNT. Death and blood! (KIT, helping ARETHUSA, has let fall the cutlass. GAUNT picks it up and runs on PEW.) Damned mutineer, I'll have your heart out! (He stops, stands staring, drops cutlass, falls upon his knees.) God forgive me! Ah, foul sins, would you blaze forth again? Lord, close your ears! Hester, Hester, hear me not! Shall all these years and tears be unavailing?

ARETHUSA. Father, I am not hurt.

GAUNT. Ay, daughter, but my soul—my lost soul!

PEW (rising on his elbow). Rum? You've done me. For God's sake, rum. (ARETHUSA pours out a glass, which KIT gives to him.) Rum? This ain't rum; it's fire! (With great excitement.) What's this? I don't like rum? (Feebly.) Ay, then, I'm a dead man, and give me water.

GAUNT. Now even his sins desert him.

PEW (drinking water). Jack Gaunt, you've always been my rock ahead. It's thanks to you I've got my papers, and this time I'm shipped for Fiddler's Green. Admiral, we ain't like to meet again, and I'll give you a toast: Here's Fiddler's Green, and damn all lubbers! (Seizing GAUNT'S arm.) I say—fair dealings, Jack!—none of that heaven business: Fiddler's Green's my port, now, ain't it?

GAUNT. David, you've hove short up, and God forbid that I deceive you. Pray, man, pray; for in the place to which you are bound there is no mercy and no hope.

PEW. Ay, my lass, you're black, but your blood's red, and I'm all a-muck with it. Pass the rum, and be damned to you. (Trying to sing)—

'Time for us to go,   Time for us—'

(He dies.)

GAUNT. But for the grace of God, there lies John Gaunt! Christopher, you have saved my child; and I, I, that was blinded with self-righteousness, have fallen. Take her, Christopher; but O, walk humbly!

CURTAIN

MACAIRE A MELODRAMATIC FARCE IN THREE ACTS

PERSONS REPRESENTED
ROBERT MACAIRE.
BERTRAND.
DUMONT, Landlord of the Auberge des Adrets.
CHARLES, a Gendarme, Dumont's supposed son.
GORIOT.
THE MARQUIS, Charles's Father.
THE BRIGADIER of Gendarmerie.
THE CURATE.
THE NOTARY.
A WAITER.
ERNESTINE, Goriot's Daughter.
ALINE.

MAIDS, PEASANTS (Male and Female), GENDARMES.

The Scene is laid in the Courtyard of the Auberge des Adrets, on the frontier of France and Savoy. The time 1800. The action occupies an interval of from twelve to fourteen hours: from four in the afternoon till about five in the morning.

NOTE. The time between the acts should be as brief as possible, and the piece played, where it is merely comic, in a vein of patter.

ACT I.

The Stage represents the courtyard of the Auberge des Adrets. It is surrounded by the buildings of the inn, with a gallery on the first story, approached, C., by a straight flight of stairs. L. C., the entrance doorway. A little in front of this, a small grated office, containing business table, brass-bound cabinet, and portable cash-box. In front, R. and L., tables and benches; one, L., partially laid for a considerable party.

SCENE I

ALINE and MAIDS; to whom FIDDLERS; afterwards DUMONT and CHARLES. As the curtain rises, the sound of the violins is heard approaching. ALINE and the inn servants, who are discovered laying the table, dance up to door L. C., to meet the FIDDLERS, who enter likewise dancing to their own music. Air: 'Haste to the Wedding.' The FIDDLERS exeunt playing into house, R. U. E. ALINE and MAIDS dance back to table, which they proceed to arrange

ALINE. Well, give me fiddles: fiddles and a wedding feast. It tickles your heart till your heels make a runaway match of it. I don't mind extra work, I don't, so long as there's fun about it. Hand me up that pile of plates. The quinces there, before the bride. Stick a pink in the Notary's glass: that's the girl he's courting.

DUMONT (entering; with CHARLES). Good girls, good girls! Charles, in ten minutes from now what happy faces will smile around that board!

CHARLES. Sir, my good fortune is complete; and most of all in this, that my happiness has made my father happy.

DUMONT. Your father? Ah, well, upon that point we shall have more to say.

CHARLES. What more remains that has not been said already? For surely, sir, there are few sons more fortunate in their father: and, since you approve of this marriage, may I not conceive you to be in that sense fortunate in your son?

DUMONT. Dear boy, there is always a variety of considerations. But the moment is ill chosen for dispute; to-night, at least, let our felicity be unalloyed. (Looking off L. C.) Our guests arrive: here is our good Curate, and here our cheerful Notary.

CHARLES. His old infirmity, I fear.

DUMONT. But Charles—dear boy!—at your wedding feast! I should have taken it unneighbourly had he come strictly sober.

SCENE II

To these, by the door L. C., the CURATE and the NOTARY, arm in arm; the latter owl-like and titubant

CURATE. Peace be on this house!

NOTARY (singing). 'Prove an excuse for the glass.'

DUMONT. Welcome, excellent neighbours! The Church and the Law.

CURATE. And you, Charles, let me hope your feelings are in solemn congruence with this momentous step.

NOTARY (digging CHARLES in the ribs). Married? Lovely bride? Prove an excuse!

DUMONT (to CURATE). I fear our friend? perhaps? as usual? eh?

CURATE. Possibly: I had not yet observed it.

DUMONT. Well, well, his heart is good.

CURATE. He doubtless meant it kindly.

NOTARY. Where's Aline?

ALINE. Coming, sir! (NOTARY makes for her.)

CURATE (capturing him). You will infallibly expose yourself to misconstruction. (To CHARLES.) Where is your commanding officer?

CHARLES. Why, sir, we have quite an alert. Information has been received from Lyons that the notorious malefactor, Robert Macaire, has broken prison, and the Brigadier is now scouring the country in his pursuit. I myself am instructed to watch the visitors to our house.

DUMONT. That will do, Charles: you may go. (Exit CHARLES.) You have considered the case I laid before you?

NOTARY. Considered a case?

DUMONT. Yes, yes. Charles, you know, Charles. Can he marry? under these untoward and peculiar circumstances, can he marry?

NOTARY. Now, lemme tell you: marriage is a contract to which there are two constracting parties. That being clear, I am prepared to argue categorically that your son Charles—who, it appears, is not your son Charles—I am prepared to argue that one party to a contract being null and void, the other party to a contract cannot by law oblige or constrain the first party to constract or bind himself to any contract, except the other party be able to see his way clearly to constract himself with him. I donno if I make myself clear?

DUMONT. No.

NOTARY. Now, lemme tell you: by applying justice of peace might possibly afford relief.

DUMONT. But how?

NOTARY. Ay, there's the rub.

DUMONT. But what am I to do? He's not my son, I tell you: Charles is not my son.

NOTARY. I know.

DUMONT. Perhaps a glass of wine would clear him?

NOTARY. That's what I want. (They go out, L. U. E.)

ALINE. And now, if you've done deranging my table, to the cellar for the wine, the whole pack of you. (Manet sola, considering table.) There: it's like a garden. If I had as sweet a table for my wedding, I would marry the Notary.

SCENE III

The Stage remains vacant. Enter, by door L. C., MACAIRE, followed by BERTRAND with bundle; in the traditional costume

MACAIRE. Good! No police.

BERTRAND (looking off, L. C.). Sold again!

MACAIRE. This is a favoured spot, Bertrand: ten minutes from the frontier: ten minutes from escape. Blessings on that frontier line! The criminal hops across, and lo! the reputable man. (Reading) 'Auberge des Adrets, by John Paul Dumont.' A table set for company; this is fate: Bertrand, are we the first arrivals? An office; a cabinet; a cash-box—aha! and a cash-box, golden within. A money-box is like a Quaker beauty: demure without, but what a figure of a woman! Outside gallery: an architectural feature I approve; I count it a convenience both for love and war: the troubadour—twang-twang; the craftsmen—(makes as if turning key.) The kitchen window: humming with cookery; truffles, before Jove! I was born for truffles. Cock your hat: meat, wine, rest, and occupation; men to gull, women to fool, and still the door open, the great unbolted door of the frontier!

BERTRAND. Macaire, I'm hungry.

MACAIRE. Bertrand, excuse me, you are a sensualist. I should have left you in the stone-yard at Lyons, and written no passport but my own. Your soul is incorporate with your stomach. Am I not hungry, too? My body, thanks to immortal Jupiter, is but the boy that holds the kite-string; my aspirations and designs swim like the kite sky-high, and overlook an empire.

BERTRAND. If I could get a full meal and a pound in my pocket I would hold my tongue.

MACAIRE. Dreams, dreams! We are what we are; and what are we? Who are you? who cares? Who am I? myself. What do we come from? an accident. What's a mother? an old woman. A father? the gentleman who beats her. What is crime? discovery. Virtue? opportunity. Politics? a pretext. Affection? an affectation. Morality? an affair of latitude. Punishment? this side the frontier. Reward? the other. Property? plunder. Business? other people's money—not mine, by God! and the end of life to live till we are hanged.

BERTRAND. Macaire, I came into this place with my tail between my legs already, and hungry besides; and then you get to flourishing, and it depresses me worse than the chaplain in the jail.

MACAIRE. What is a chaplain? A man they pay to say what you don't want to hear.

BERTRAND. And who are you after all? and what right have you to talk like that? By what I can hear, you've been the best part of your life in quod; and as for me, since I've followed you, what sort of luck have I had? Sold again! A boose, a blue fright, two years' hard, and the police hot-foot after us even now.

MACAIRE. What is life? A boose and the police.

BERTRAND. Of course, I know you're clever; I admire you down to the ground, and I'll starve without you. But I can't stand it, and I'm off. Good-bye: good luck to you, old man! and if you want the bundle—

MACAIRE. I am a gentleman of a mild disposition and, I thank my maker, elegant manners; but rather than be betrayed by such a thing as you are, with the courage of a hare, and the manners, by the Lord Harry, of a jumping-Jack—(He shows his knife.)

BERTRAND. Put it up, put it up: I'll do what you want.

MACAIRE. What is obedience? fear. So march straight, or look for mischief. It's not bon ton, I know, and far from friendly. But what is friendship? convenience. But we lose time in this amiable dalliance. Come, now an effort of deportment: the head thrown back, a jaunty carriage of the leg; crook gracefully the elbow. Thus. 'Tis better. (Calling.) House, house here!

BERTRAND. Are you mad? We haven't a brass farthing.

MACAIRE. Now!—But before we leave!

SCENE IV

To these, DUMONT

DUMONT. Gentlemen, what can a plain man do for your service?

MACAIRE. My good man, in a roadside inn one cannot look for the impossible. Give one what small wine and what country fare you can produce.

DUMONT. Gentlemen, you come here upon a most auspicious day, a red-letter day for me and my poor house, when all are welcome. Suffer me, with all delicacy, to inquire if you are not in somewhat narrow circumstances?

MACAIRE. My good creature, you are strangely in error; one is rolling in gold.

BERTRAND. And very hungry.

DUMONT. Dear me, and on this happy occasion I had registered a vow that every poor traveller should have his keep for nothing, and a pound in his pocket to help him on his journey.

MACAIRE (aside). A pound in his pocket?

BERTRAND (aside). Keep for nothing?

MACAIRE (aside). Bitten!

BERTRAND (aside). Sold again!

DUMONT. I will send you what we have: poor fare, perhaps, for gentlemen like you.

SCENE V

MACAIRE, BERTRAND; afterwards CHARLES, who appears on the gallery, and comes down

BERTRAND. I told you so. Why will you fly so high?

MACAIRE. Bertrand, don't crush me. A pound: a fortune! With a pound to start upon—two pounds, for I'd have borrowed yours—three months from now I might have been driving in my barouche, with you behind it, Bertrand, in a tasteful livery.

BERTRAND (seeing CHARLES). Lord, a policeman!

MACAIRE. Steady! What is a policeman? Justice's blind eye. (To CHARLES.) I think, sir, you are in the force?

CHARLES. I am, sir, and it was in that character—

MACAIRE. Ah, sir, a fine service!

CHARLES. It is, sir, and if your papers—

MACAIRE. You become your uniform. Have you a mother? Ah, well, well!

CHARLES. My duty, sir—

MACAIRE. They tell me one Macaire—is not that his name, Bertrand?—has broken jail at Lyons?

CHARLES. He has, sir, and it is precisely for that reason—

MACAIRE. Well, good-bye. (Shaking CHARLES by the hand and leading him towards the door, L. U. E.) Sweet spot, sweet spot. The scenery is . . . (kisses his finger-tips. Exit CHARLES). And now, what is a policeman?

BERTRAND. A bobby.

SCENE VI

MACAIRE, BERTRAND; to whom ALINE with tray; and afterwards MAIDS

ALINE (entering with tray, and proceeding to lay table, L.) My men, you are in better luck than usual. It isn't every day you go shares in a wedding feast.

MACAIRE. A wedding? Ah, and you're the bride.

ALINE. What makes you fancy that?

MACAIRE. Heavens, am I blind?

ALINE. Well, then, I wish I was.

MACAIRE. I take you at the word: have me.

ALINE. You will never be hanged for modesty.

MACAIRE. Modesty is for the poor: when one is rich and nobly born, 'tis but a clog. I love you. What is your name?

ALINE. Guess again, and you'll guess wrong. (Enter the other servants with wine baskets.) Here, set the wine down. No, that is the old Burgundy for the wedding party. These gentlemen must put up with a different bin. (Setting wine before MACAIRE and BERTRAND, who are at table, L.)

MACAIRE (drinking). Vinegar, by the supreme Jove!

BERTRAND. Sold again!

MACAIRE. Now, Bertrand, mark me. (Before the servants he exchanges the bottle for the one in front of DUMONT'S place at the head of the other table.) Was it well done?

BERTRAND. Immense.

MACAIRE (emptying his glass into BERTRAND'S). There, Bertrand, you may finish that. Ha! music?

SCENE VII

To these, from the inn, L. U. E., DUMONT, CHARLES, the CURATE, the NOTARY jigging: from the inn, R. U. E., FIDDLERS playing and dancing; and through door L. C., GORIOT, ERNESTINE, PEASANTS, dancing likewise. Air: 'Haste to the Wedding.' As the parties meet, the music ceases

DUMONT. Welcome, neighbours! welcome friends! Ernestine, here is my Charles, no longer mine. A thousand welcomes. O the gay day! O the auspicious wedding! (CHARLES, ERNESTINE, DUMONT, GORIOT, CURATE, and NOTARY sit to the wedding feast; PEASANTS, FIDDLERS, and MAIDS, grouped at back, drinking from the barrel.) O, I must have all happy around me.

GORIOT. Then help the soup.

DUMONT. Give me leave: I must have all happy. Shall these poor gentlemen upon a day like this drink ordinary wine? Not so: I shall drink it. (To MACAIRE, who is just about to fill his glass) Don't touch it, sir! Aline, give me that gentleman's bottle and take him mine: with old Dumont's compliments.

MACAIRE. What?

BERTRAND. Change the bottle?

MACAIRE (aside). Bitten!

BERTRAND (aside). Sold again.

DUMONT. Yes, all shall be happy.

GORIOT. I tell 'ee, help the soup!

DUMONT (begins to help soup. Then, dropping ladle.) One word: a matter of detail: Charles is not my son. (All exclaim.) O no, he is not my son. Perhaps I should have mentioned it before.

CHARLES. I am not your son, sir?

DUMONT. O no, far from it.

GORIOT. Then who the devil's son be he?

DUMONT. O, I don't know. It's an odd tale, a romantic tale: it may amuse you. It was twenty years ago, when I kept the Golden Head at Lyons: Charles was left upon my doorstep in a covered basket, with sufficient money to support the child till he should come of age. There was no mark upon the linen, nor any clue but one: an unsigned letter from the father of the child, which he strictly charged me to preserve. It was to prove his identity: he, of course, would know the contents, and he only; so I keep it safe in the third compartment of my cash-box, with the ten thousand francs I've saved for his dowry. Here is the key; it's a patent key. To-day the poor boy is twenty-one, to-morrow to be married. I did perhaps hope the father would appear: there was a Marquis coming; he wrote me for a room; I gave him the best, Number Thirteen, which you have all heard of: I did hope it might be he, for a Marquis, you know, is always genteel. But no, you see. As for me, I take you all to witness I'm as innocent of him as the babe unborn.

MACAIRE. Ahem! I think you said the linen bore an M?

DUMONT. Pardon me: the markings were cut off.

MACAIRE. True. The basket white, I think?

DUMONT. Drown, brown.

MACAIRE. Ah! brown—a whitey-brown.

GORIOT. I tell 'ee what, Dumont, this is all very well; but in that case, I'll be danged if he gets my daater. (General consternation.)

DUMONT. O Goriot, let's have happy faces!

GORIOT. Happy faces be danged! I want to marry my daater; I want your son. But who be this? I don't know, and you don't know, and he don't know. He may be anybody; by Jarge, he may be nobody! (Exclamations.)

CURATE. The situation is crepuscular.

ERNESTINE. Father, and Mr. Dumont (and you too, Charles), I wish to say one word. You gave us leave to fall in love; we fell in love; and as for me, my father, I will either marry Charles, or die a maid.

CHARLES. And you, sir, would you rob me in one day of both a father and a wife?

DUMONT (weeping). Happy faces, happy faces!

GORIOT. I know nothing about robbery; but she cannot marry without my consent, and that she cannot get.

(All speak together . . .

DUMONT. O dear, O dear!

ALINE. What spoil the wedding?

ERNESTINE. O father!

CHARLES. Sir, sir, you would not—

GORIOT (exasperated). I wun't, and what's more I shan't.

NOTARY. I donno if I make myself clear?

DUMONT. Goriot, do let's have happy faces!

GORIOT. Fudge! Fudge!! Fudge!!!

CURATE. Possibly on application to this conscientious jurist, light may be obtained.

ALL. The Notary; yes, yes; the Notary!

DUMONT. Now, how about this marriage?

NOTARY. Marriage is a contract, to which there are two constracting parties, John Doe and Richard Roe. I donno if I make myself clear?

ALINE. Poor lamb!

CURATE. Silence, my friend; you will expose yourself to misconstruction.

MACAIRE (taking the stage). As an entire stranger in this painful scene, will you permit a gentleman and a traveller to interject one word? There sits the young man, full, I am sure, of pleasing qualities; here the young maiden, by her own confession bashfully consenting to the match; there sits that dear old gentleman, a lover of bright faces like myself, his own now dimmed with sorrow; and here—(may I be allowed to add?)—here sits this noble Roman, a father like myself, and like myself the slave of duty. Last you have me—Baron Henri-Frédéric de Latour de Main de la Tonnerre de Brest, the man of the world and the man of delicacy. I find you all—permit me the expression—gravelled. A marriage and an obstacle. Now, what is marriage? The union of two souls, and, what is possibly more romantic, the fusion of two dowries. What is an obstacle? the devil. And this obstacle? to me, as a man of family, the obstacle seems grave; but to me, as a man and a brother, what is it but a word? O my friend (to GORIOT), you whom I single out as the victim of the same noble failings with myself—of pride of birth, of pride of honesty—O my friend, reflect. Go now apart with your dishevelled daughter, your tearful son-in-law, and let their plaints constrain you. Believe me, when you come to die, you will recall with pride this amiable weakness.

GORIOT. I shan't, and what's more I wun't. (CHARLES and ERNESTINE lead him up stage, protesting. All rise, except NOTARY.)

DUMONT (front R., shaking hands with MACAIRE). Sir, you have a noble nature. (MACAIRE picks his pocket.) Dear me, dear me, and you are rich.

MACAIRE. I own, sir, I deceived you: I feared some wounding offer, and my pride replied. But to be quite frank with you, you behold me here, the Baron Henri-Frédéric de Latour de Main de la Tonnerre de Brest, and between my simple manhood and the infinite these rags are all.

DUMONT. Dear me, and with this noble pride, my gratitude is useless. For I, too, have delicacy: I understand you could not stoop to take a gift.

MACAIRE. A gift? a small one? never!

DUMONT. And I will never wound you by the offer.

MACAIRE (aside). Bitten.

BERTRAND (aside). Sold again.

GORIOT (taking the stage). But, look'ee here, he can't marry.

(All speak together . . .

MACAIRE. Hey?

DUMONT. Ah!

ALINE. Hey day!

CURATE. Wherefore?

ERNESTINE. Oh!

CHARLES. Ah!

GORIOT. Not without his veyther's consent! And he hasn't got it; and what's more, he can't get it: and what's more, he hasn't got a veyther to get it from. It's the law of France.

ALINE. Then the law of France ought to be ashamed of itself.

ERNESTINE. O, couldn't we ask the Notary again?

CURATE. Indubitably you may ask him.

(All speak together . . .

MACAIRE. Can't they marry?

DUMONT. Can't he marry?

ALINE. Can't she marry?

ERNESTINE. Can't we marry?

CHARLES. Can't I marry?

GORIOT. Bain't I right?

NOTARY. Constracting parties.

CURATE. Possibly to-morrow at an early hour he may be more perspicuous.

GORIOT. Ay, before he've time to get at it.

NOTARY. Unoffending jurisconsult overtaken by sorrow. Possibly by applying justice of peace might afford relief.

(All speak together . . .

MACAIRE. Bravo!

DUMONT. Excellent!

CHARLES. Let's go at once!

ALINE. The very thing!

ERNESTINE. Yes, this minute!

GORIOT. I'll go. I don't mind getting advice, but I wun't take it.

MACAIRE. My friends, one word: I perceive by your downcast looks that you have not recognised the true nature of your responsibility as citizens of time. What is care? impiety. Joy? the whole duty of man. Here is an opportunity of duty it were sinful to forego. With a word, I could lighten your hearts; but I prefer to quicken your heels, and send you forth on your ingenuous errand with happy faces and smiling thoughts, the physicians of your own recovery. Fiddlers, to your catgut! Up, Bertrand, and show them how one foots it in society; forward, girls, and choose me every one the lad she loves; Dumont, benign old man, lead forth our blushing Curate; and you, O bride, embrace the uniform of your beloved, and help us dance in your wedding-day. (Dance, in the course of which MACAIRE picks DUMONT'S pocket of his keys, selects the key of the cash-box, and returns the others to his pocket. In the end, all dance out: the wedding-party, headed by FIDDLERS, L. C.; the MAIDS and ALINE into the inn, R. U. E. Manet BERTRAND and MACAIRE.)

SCENE VIII

MACAIRE, BERTRAND, who instantly takes a bottle from the wedding-table, and sits with it, L.

MACAIRE. Bertrand, there's a devil of a want of a father here.

BERTRAND. Ay, if we only knew where to find him.

MACAIRE. Bertrand, look at me: I am Macaire; I am that father.

BERTRAND. You, Macaire? you a father?

MACAIRE. Not yet, but in five minutes. I am capable of anything. (Producing key.) What think you of this?

BERTRAND. That? Is it a key?

MACAIRE. Ay, boy, and what besides? my diploma of respectability, my patent of fatherhood. I prigged it—in the ardour of the dance I prigged it; I change it beyond recognition, thus (twists the handle of the key); and now . . .? Where is my long-lost child? produce my young policeman! show me my gallant boy!

BERTRAND. I don't understand.

MACAIRE. Dear innocence, how should you? Your brains are in your fists. Go and keep watch. (He goes into the office and returns with the cash-box.) Keep watch, I say.

BERTRAND. Where?

MACAIRE. Everywhere. (He opens box.)

BERTRAND. Gold.

MACAIRE. Hands off! Keep watch. (BERTRAND at back of stage.) Beat slower, my paternal heart! The third compartment; let me see.

BERTRAND. S'st! (MACAIRE shuts box.) No; false alarm.

MACAIRE. The third compartment. Ay, here t—

BERTRAND. S'st! (Same business.) No: fire away.

MACAIRE. The third compartment: it must be this.

BERTRAND. S'st! (MACAIRE, keeps box open, watching BERTRAND.) All serene; it's the wind.

MACAIRE. Now, see here! (He darts his knife into the stage.) I will either be backed as a man should be, or from this minute out I'll work alone. Do you understand? I said alone.

BERTRAND. For the Lord's sake, Macaire!—

MACAIRE. Ay, here it is. (Reading letter). 'Preserve this letter secretly; its terms are known only to you and me: hence when the time comes, I shall repeat them, and my son will recognise his father.' Signed: 'Your Unknown Benefactor.' (He turns it over twice and replaces it. Then, fingering the gold) Gold! The yellow enchantress, happiness ready-made and laughing in my face! Gold: what is gold? The world; the term of ills; the empery of all; the multitudinous babble of the change, the sailing from all ports of freighted argosies; music, wine, a palace; the doors of the bright theatre, the key of consciences, and love—love's whistle! All this below my itching fingers; and to set this by, turn a deaf ear upon the siren present, and condescend once more, naked, into the ring with fortune—Macaire, how few would do it! But you, Macaire, you are compacted of more subtle clay. No cheap immediate pilfering: no retail trade of petty larceny; but swoop at the heart of the position, and clutch all!

BERTRAND (at his shoulder). Halves!

MACAIRE. Halves? (He locks the box.) Bertrand, I am a father. (Replaces box in office.)

BERTRAND (looking after him). Well, I—am—damned!

ACT - CURTAIN DROP.

ACT II.

When the curtain rises, the night has come. A hanging cluster of lighted lamps over each table, R. and L. MACAIRE, R., smoking a cigarette; BERTRAND, L., with a church-warden: each with bottle and glass

SCENE I

MACAIRE, BERTRAND

MACAIRE. Bertrand, I am content: a child might play with me. Does your pipe draw well?

BERTRAND. Like a factory chimney. This is my notion of life: liquor, a chair, a table to put my feet on, a fine clean pipe, and no police.

MACAIRE. Bertrand, do you see these changing exhalations? do you see these blue rings and spirals, weaving their dance, like a round of fairies, on the footless air?

BERTRAND. I see 'em right enough.

MACAIRE. Man of little vision, expound me these meteors! what do they signify, O wooden-head? Clod, of what do they consist?

BERTRAND. Damned bad tobacco.

MACAIRE. I will give you a little course of science. Everything, Bertrand (much as it may surprise you), has three states: a vapour, a liquid, a solid. These are fortune in the vapour: these are ideas. What are ideas? the protoplasm of wealth. To your head—which, by the way, is a solid, Bertrand—what are they but foul air? To mine, to my prehensile and constructive intellects, see, as I grasp and work them, to what lineaments of the future they transform themselves: a palace, a barouche, a pair of luminous footmen, plate, wine, respect, and to be honest!

BERTRAND. But what's the sense in honesty?

MACAIRE. The sense? You see me: Macaire: elegant, immoral, invincible in cunning; well, Bertrand, much as it may surprise you, I am simply damned by my dishonesty.

BERTRAND. No!

MACAIRE. The honest man, Bertrand, that God's noblest work. He carries the bag, my boy. Would you have me define honesty? the strategic point for theft. Bertrand, if I'd three hundred a year, I'd be honest to-morrow.

BERTRAND. Ah! Don't you wish you may get it!

MACAIRE. Bertrand, I will bet you my head against your own—the longest odds I can imagine—that with honesty for my spring-board, I leap through history like a paper hoop, and come out among posterity heroic and immortal.

SCENE II

To these, all the former characters, less the NOTARY. The fiddles are heard without, playing dolefully. Air: 'O dear, what can the matter be?' in time to which the procession enters

MACAIRE. Well, friends, what cheer?

(All speak together . . .

ALINE. No wedding, no wedding!

GORIOT. I told 'ee he can't and he can't.

DUMONT. Dear, dear me!

ERNESTINE. They won't let us marry.

CHARLES. No wife, no father, no nothing!

CURATE. The facts have justified the worst anticipations of our absent friend, the Notary.

MACAIRE. I perceive I must reveal myself.

DUMONT. God bless me, no!

MACAIRE. My friends, I had meant to preserve a strict incognito, for I was ashamed (I own it!) of this poor accoutrement; but when I see a face that I can render happy, say, my old Dumont, should I hesitate to work the change? Hear me, then, and you (to the others) prepare a smiling countenance. (Repeating.) 'Preserve this letter secretly; its terms are only known to you and me; hence when the time comes, I shall repeat them, and my son will recognise his father.—Your Unknown Benefactor.'

DUMONT. The words! the letter! Charles, alas! it is your father!

CHARLES. Good Lord! (General consternation.)

BERTRAND (aside: smiling his brow). I see it now; sublime!

CURATE. A highly singular eventuality.

GORIOT. Him? O well, then, I wun't. (Goes up.)

MACAIRE. Charles, to my arms! (Business.) Ernestine, your second father waits to welcome you. (Business.) Goriot, noble old man, I grasp your hand. (He doesn't.) And you, Dumont, how shall your unknown benefactor thank you for your kindness to his boy? (A dead Pause.) Charles, to my arms!

CHARLES. My father, you are still something of a stranger. I hope—er—in the course of time—I hope that may be somewhat mended. But I confess that I have so long regarded Mr. Dumont—

MACAIRE. Love him still, dear boy, love him still. I have not returned to be a burden on your heart, nor much, comparatively, on your pocket. A place by the fire, dear boy, a crust for my friend, Bertrand. (A dead pause.) Ah, well, this is a different home-coming from that I fancied when I left the letter: I dreamed to grow rich. Charles, you remind me of your sainted mother.

CHARLES. I trust, sir, you do not think yourself less welcome for your poverty.

MACAIRE. Nay, nay—more welcome, more welcome. O, I know your—(business) backs! Besides, my poverty is noble. Political . . . Dumont, what are your politics?

DUMONT. A plain old republican, my lord.

MACAIRE. And yours, my good Goriot?

GORIOT. I be a royalist, I be, and so be my daater.

MACAIRE. How strange is the coincidence! The party that I sought to found combined the peculiarities of both: a patriotic enterprise in which I fell. This humble fellow . . . have I introduced him? You behold in us the embodiment of aristocracy and democracy. Bertrand, shake hands with my family. (BERTRAND is rebuffed by one and the other in dead silence.)

BERTRAND. Sold again!

MACAIRE. Charles, to my arms! (Business.)

ERNESTINE. Well, but now that he has a father of some kind, cannot the marriage go on?

MACAIRE. Angel, this very night: I burn to take my grandchild on my knees.

GORIOT. Be you that young man's veyther?

MACAIRE. Ay, and what a father!

GORIOT. Then all I've got to say is, I shan't and I wun't.

MACAIRE. Ah, friends, friends, what a satisfaction it is, what a sight is virtue! I came among you in this poor attire to test you; how nobly have you borne the test! But my disguise begins to irk me: who will lend me a good suit? (Business.)

SCENE III

To these, the MARQUIS, L. C.

MARQUIS. Is this the house of John Paul Dumont, once of Lyons?

DUMONT. It is, sir, and I am he, at your disposal.

MARQUIS. I am the Marquis Villers-Cotterêts de la Cherté de Médoc. (Sensation.)

MACAIRE. Marquis, delighted, I am sure.

MARQUIS (to DUMONT). I come, as you perceive, unfollowed; my errand, therefore, is discreet. I come (producing notes from breast-pocket) equipped with thirty thousand francs; my errand, therefore, must be generous. Can you not guess?

DUMONT. Not I, my lord.

MARQUIS (repeating). 'Preserve this letter,' etc.

MACAIRE. Bitten.

BERTRAND. Sold again (aside). (A pause.)

ALINE. Well, I never did!

DUMONT. Two fathers!

MARQUIS. Two? Impossible.

DUMONT. Not at all. This is the other.

MARQUIS. This man?

MACAIRE. This is the man, my lord; here stands the father; Charles, to my arms! (CHARLES backs.)

DUMONT. He knew the letter.

MARQUIS. Well, but so did I.

CURATE. The judgment of Solomon.

GORIOT. What did I tell 'ee? he can't marry.

ERNESTINE. Couldn't they both consent?

MARQUIS. But he's my living image.

MACAIRE. Mine, Marquis, mine.

MARQUIS. My figure, I think?

MACAIRE. Ah, Charles, Charles!

CURATE. We used to think his physiognomy resembled Dumont's.

DUMONT. Come to look at him, he's really like Goriot.

ERNESTINE. O papa, I hope he's not my brother.

GORIOT. What be talking of? I tell 'ee, he's like our Curate.

CHARLES. Gentlemen, my head aches.

MARQUIS. I have it: the involuntary voice of nature. Look at me, my son.

MACAIRE. Nay, Charles, but look at me.

CHARLES. Gentlemen, I am unconscious of the smallest natural inclination for either.

MARQUIS. Another thought: what was his mother's name?

MACAIRE. What was the name of his mother by you?

MARQUIS. Sir, you are silenced.

MACAIRE. Silenced by honour. I had rather lose my boy than compromise his sainted mother.

MARQUIS. A thought: twins might explain it: had you not two foundlings?

DUMONT. Nay, sir, one only; and judging by the miseries of this evening, I should say, thank God!

MACAIRE. My friends, leave me alone with the Marquis. It is only a father that can understand a father's heart. Bertrand, follow the members of my family. (They troop out, L. U. E. and R. U. E., the fiddlers playing. Air: 'O dear, what can the matter be?')

SCENE IV

MACAIRE, MARQUIS

MARQUIS. Well, sir?

MACAIRE. My lord, I feel for you. (Business. They sit, R.)

MARQUIS. And now, sir?

MACAIRE. The bond that joins us is remarkable and touching.

MARQUIS. Well, sir?

MACAIRE (touching him on the breast). You have there thirty thousand francs.

MARQUIS. Well, sir?

MACAIRE. I was but thinking of the inequalities of life, my lord: that I who, for all you know, may be the father of your son, should have nothing; and that you who, for all I know, may be the father of mine, should be literally bulging with bank notes. . . . Where do you keep them at night?

MARQUIS. Under my pillow. I think it rather ingenious.

MACAIRE. Admirably so! I applaud the device.

MARQUIS. Well, sir?

MACAIRE. Do you snuff, my lord?

MARQUIS. No, sir, I do not.

MACAIRE. My lord, I am a poor man.

MARQUIS. Well, sir? and what of that?

MACAIRE. The affections, my lord, are priceless. Money will not buy them; or, at least, it takes a great deal.

MARQUIS. Sir, your sentiments do you honour.

MACAIRE. My lord, you are rich.

MARQUIS. Well, sir?

MACAIRE. Now follow me, I beseech you. Here am I, my lord; and there, if I may so express myself, are you. Each has the father's heart, and there we are equal; each claims yon interesting lad, and there again we are on a par. But, my lord—and here we come to the inequality, and what I consider the unfairness of the thing—you have thirty thousand francs, and I, my lord, have not a rap. You mark me? not a rap, my lord! My lord, put yourself in my position: consider what must be my feelings, my desires; and—hey?

MARQUIS. I fail to grasp . . .

MACAIRE (with irritation). My dear man, there is the door of the house; here am I; there (touching, MARQUIS on the breast) are thirty thousand francs. Well, now?

MARQUIS. I give you my word of honour, sir, I gather nothing; my mind is quite unused to such prolonged exertion. If the boy be yours, he is not mine; if he be mine, he is not yours; and if he is neither of ours, or both of ours . . . in short, my mind . . .

MACAIRE. My lord, will you lay those thirty thousand francs upon the table?

MARQUIS. I fail to grasp . . . but if it will in any way oblige you . . . (Does so.)

MACAIRE. Now, my lord, follow me: I take them up; you see? I put them in my pocket; you follow me? This is my hat; here is my stick; and here is my—my friend's bundle.

MARQUIS. But that is my cloak.

MACAIRE. Precisely. Now, my lord, one more effort of your lordship's mind. If I were to go out of that door, with the full intention—follow me close—the full intention of never being heard of more, what would you do?

MARQUIS. I!—send for the police.

MACAIRE. Take your money! (Dashing down the notes.) Man, if I met you in a lane! (He drops his head upon the table.)

MARQUIS. The poor soul is insane. The other man, whom I suppose to be his keeper, is very much to blame.

MACAIRE (raising his head). I have a light! (To MARQUIS.) With invincible oafishness, my lord, I cannot struggle. I pass you by; I leave you gaping by the wayside; I blush to have a share in the progeny of such an owl. Off, off, and send the tapster!

MARQUIS. Poor fellow!

SCENE V

MACAIRE, to whom BERTRAND. Afterwards DUMONT

BERTRAND. Well?

MACAIRE. Bitten.

BERTRAND. Sold again.

MACAIRE. Had he the wit of a lucifer match! But what can gods or men against stupidity? Still, I have a trick. Where is that damned old man?

DUMONT (entering). I hear you want me.

MACAIRE. Ah, my good old Dumont, this is very sad.

DUMONT. Dear me, what is wrong?

MACAIRE. Dumont, you had a dowry for my son?

DUMONT. I had; I have: ten thousand francs.

MACAIRE. It's a poor thing, but it must do. Dumont, I bury my old hopes, my old paternal tenderness.

DUMONT. What? is he not your son?

MACAIRE. Pardon me, my friend. The Marquis claims my boy. I will not seek to deny that he attempted to corrupt me, or that I spurned his gold. It was thirty thousand.

DUMONT. Noble soul!

MACAIRE. One has a heart . . . He spoke, Dumont, that proud noble spoke, of the advantages to our beloved Charles; and in my father's heart a voice arose, louder than thunder. Dumont, was I unselfish? The voice said no; the voice, Dumont, up and told me to begone.

DUMONT. To begone? to go?

MACAIRE. To begone, Dumont, and to go. Both, Dumont. To leave my son to marry, and be rich and happy as the son of another; to creep forth myself, old, penniless, broken-hearted, exposed to the inclemencies of heaven and the rebuffs of the police.

DUMONT. This is what I had looked for at your hands. Noble, nobleman!

MACAIRE. One has a heart . . . and yet, Dumont, it can hardly have escaped your penetration that if I were to shift from this hostelry without a farthing, and leave my offspring to wallow—literally—among millions, I should play the part of little better than an ass.

DUMONT. But I had thought . . . I had fancied . . .

MACAIRE. No, Dumont, you had not; do not seek to impose upon my simplicity. What you did think was this, Dumont: for the sake of this noble father, for the sake of this son whom he denies for his own interest—I mean, for his interest—no, I mean, for his own—well, anyway, in order to keep up the general atmosphere of sacrifice and nobility, I must hand over this dowry to the Baron Henri-Frédéric de Latour de Main de la Tonnerre de Brest.

(Together: each shaking him by the hand . . .

DUMONT. Noble, O noble!

BERTRAND. Beautiful, O beautiful!

DUMONT. Now Charles is rich he needs it not. For whom could it more fittingly be set aside than for his noble father? I will give it you at once.

BERTRAND. At once, at once!

MACAIRE (aside to BERTRAND). Hang on. (Aloud.) Charles, Charles, my lost boy! (He falls weeping at L. table. DUMONT enters the office, and brings down cash-box to table R. He feels in all his pockets: BERTRAND from behind him making signs to MACAIRE, which the latter does not see.)

DUMONT. That's strange. I can't find the key. It's a patent key.

BERTRAND (behind DUMONT, making signs to MACAIRE). The key, he can't find the key.

MACAIRE. O yes, I remember. I heard it drop. (Drops key.) And here it is before my eyes.

DUMONT. That? That's yours. I saw it drop.

MACAIRE. I give you my word of honour I heard it fall five minutes back.

DUMONT. But I saw it.

MACAIRE. Impossible. It must be yours.

DUMONT. It is like mine, indeed. How came it in your pocket?

MACAIRE. Bitten. (Aside.)

BERTRAND. Sold again (aside) . . . You forget, Baron, it's the key of my valise; I gave it you to keep in consequence of the hole in my pocket.

MACAIRE. True, true; and that explains.

DUMONT. O, that explains. Now, all we have to do is to find mine. It's a patent key. You heard it drop.

MACAIRE. Distinctly.

BERTRAND. So I did: distinctly.

DUMONT. Here, Aline, Babette, Goriot, Curate, Charles, everybody, come here and look for my key!

SCENE VI

To these with candles, all the former characters, except FIDDLERS, PEASANTS, and NOTARY. They hunt for the key

DUMONT. It's bound to be here. We all heard it drop.

MARQUIS (with BERTRAND'S bundle). Is this it?

ALL (with fury). No.

BERTRAND. Hands off, that's my luggage. (Hunt resumed.)

DUMONT. I heard it drop, as plain as ever I heard anything.

MARQUIS. By the way (all start up), what are we looking for?

ALL (with fury). O!!

DUMONT. Will you have the kindness to find my key? (Hunt resumed.)

CURATE. What description of a key—

DUMONT. A patent, patent, patent, patent key!

MACAIRE. I have it. Here it is!

ALL (with relief). Ah!!

DUMONT. That? What do you mean? That's yours.

MACAIRE. Pardon me.

DUMONT. It is.

MACAIRE. It isn't.

DUMONT. I tell you it is: look at that twisted handle.

MACAIRE. It can't be mine, and so it must be yours.

DUMONT. It is not. Feel in your pockets. (To the others.) Will you have the kindness to find my patent key?

ALL. Oh!! (Hunt resumed.)

MACAIRE. Ah, well, you're right. (He slips key into DUMONT'S pocket.) An idea: suppose you felt in your pocket?

ALL (rising). Yes! Suppose you did!

DUMONT. I will not feel in my pockets. How could it be there? It's a patent key. This is more than any man can bear. First, Charles is one man's son, and then he's another's, and then he's nobody's, and be damned to him! And then there's my key lost; and then there's your key! What is your key? Where is your key? Where isn't it? And why is it like mine, only mine's a patent? The long and short of it is this: that I'm going to bed, and that you're all going to bed, and that I refuse to hear another word upon the subject or upon any subject. There!

MACAIRE (aside). Bitten.

BERTRAND (aside). Sold again.

(ALINE and MAIDS extinguish hanging lamps over tables, R. and L. Stage lighted only by guests' candles.)

CHARLES. But, sir, I cannot decently retire to rest till I embrace my honoured parent. Which is it to be?

MACAIRE. Charles, to my—

DUMONT. Embrace neither of them; embrace nobody; there has been too much of this sickening folly. To bed!!! (Exit violently R. U. E. All the characters troop slowly upstairs, talking in dumb show. BERTRAND and MACAIRE remain in front C., watching them go.)

BERTRAND. Sold again, captain?

MACAIRE. Ay, they will have it.

BERTRAND. It? What?

MACAIRE. The worst, Bertrand. What is man? a beast of prey. An hour ago, and I'd have taken a crust, and gone in peace. But no: they would trick and juggle, curse them; they would wriggle and cheat! Well, I accept the challenge: war to the knife.

BERTRAND. Murder?

MACAIRE. What is murder? A legal term for a man dying. Call it Fate, and that's philosophy; call me Providence, and you talk religion. Die? My, that is what man is made for; we are full of mortal parts; we are all as good as dead already, we hang so close upon the brink: touch a button, and the strongest falls in dissolution. Now, see how easy: I take you—(grappling him.)

BERTRAND. Macaire—O no!

MACAIRE. Fool! would I harm a fly, when I had nothing to gain? As the butcher with the sheep, I kill to live; and where is the difference between man and mutton? pride and a tailor's bill. Murder? I know who made that name—a man crouching from the knife! Selfishness made it—the aggregated egotism called society; but I meet that with a selfishness as great. Has he money? Have I none—great powers, none? Well, then, I fatten and manure my life with his.

BERTRAND. You frighten me. Who is it?

MACAIRE. Mark well. (The MARQUIS opens the door of Number Thirteen, and the rest, clustering round, bid him good-night. As they begin to disperse along the gallery he enters and shuts the door.) Out, out, brief candle! That man is doomed.

ACT - CURTAIN DROP.

ACT III

SCENE I

MACAIRE, BERTRAND

As the curtain rises, the stage is dark and empty. Enter MACAIRE, L. U. E., with lantern. He looks about

MACAIRE (calling off). S'st!

BERTRAND (entering L. U. E.). It's creeping dark.

MACAIRE. Blinding dark; and a good job.

BERTRAND. Macaire, I'm cold; my very hair's cold.

MACAIRE. Work, work will warm you: to your keys.

BERTRAND. No, Macaire, it's a horror. You not kill him; let's have no bloodshed.

MACAIRE. None: it spoils your clothes. Now, see: you have keys and you have experience; up that stair, and pick me the lock of that man's door. Pick me the lock of that man's door.

BERTRAND. May I take the light?

MACAIRE. You may not. Go. (BERTRAND mounts the stairs, and is seen picking the lock of Number Thirteen.) The earth spins eastward, and the day is at the door. Yet half an hour of covert, and the sun will be afoot, the discoverer, the great policeman. Yet, half an hour of night, the good, hiding, practicable night; and lo! at a touch the gas-jet of the universe turned on; and up with the sun gets the providence of honest people, puts off his night-cap, throws up his window, stares out of house— and the rogue must skulk again till dusk. Yet half an hour and, Macaire, you shall be safe and rich. If yon fool—my fool—would but miscarry, if the dolt within would hear and leap upon him, I could intervene, kill both, by heaven—both!—cry murder with the best, and at one stroke reap honour and gold. For, Bertrand dead—

BERTRAND (from above). S'st, Macaire!

MACAIRE. Is it done, dear boy? Come down. (BERTRAND descends.) Sit down beside this light: this is your ring of safety, budge not beyond—the night is crowded with hobgoblins. See ghosts and tremble like a jelly if you must; but remember men are my concern; and at the creak of a man's foot, hist! (Sharpening his knife upon his sleeve.) What is a knife? A plain man's sword.

BERTRAND. Not the knife, Macaire; O, not the knife!

MACAIRE. My name is Self-Defence. (He goes upstairs and enters Number Thirteen.)

BERTRAND. He's in. I hear a board creak. What a night, what a night! Will he hear him? O Lord, my poor Macaire! I hear nothing, nothing. The night's as empty as a dream: he must hear him; he cannot help but hear him; and then—O Macaire, Macaire, come back to me. It's death, and it's death, and it's death. Red, red: a corpse. Macaire to kill, Macaire to die? I'd rather starve, I'd rather perish, than either: I'm not fit, I'm not fit, for either! Why, how's this? I want to cry. (A stroke, and groan from above.) God Almighty, one of them's gone! (He falls with his head on table, R. MACAIRE appears at the top of the stairs, descends, comes airily forward and touches him on the shoulder. BERTRAND, with a cry, turns and falls upon his neck.) O, O, and I thought I had lost him. (Day breaking.)

MACAIRE. The contrary, dear boy. (He produces notes.)

BERTRAND. What was it like?

MACAIRE. Like? Nothing. A little blood, a dead man.

BERTRAND. Blood! . . . Dead! He falls at table sobbing. MACAIRE divides the notes into two parts; on the smaller he wipes the bloody knife, and folding the stains inward, thrusts the notes into BERTRAND'S face.)

MACAIRE. What is life without the pleasures of the table!

BERTRAND (taking and pocketing notes). Macaire, I can't get over it.

MACAIRE. My mark is the frontier, and at top speed. Don't hang your jaw at me. Up, up, at the double; pick me that cash-box; and let's get the damned house fairly cleared.

BERTRAND. I can't. Did he bleed much?

MACAIRE. Bleed? Must I bleed you? To work, or I'm dangerous.

BERTRAND. It's all right, Macaire; I'm going.

MACAIRE. Better so: an old friend is nearly sacred. (Full daylight: lights up. MACAIRE blows out lantern.)

BERTRAND. Where's the key?

MACAIRE. Key? I tell you to pick it.

BERTRAND (with the box). But it's a patent lock. Where is the key? You had it.

MACAIRE. Will you pick that lock?

BERTRAND. I can't: it's a patent. Where's the key?

MACAIRE. If you will have it, I put it back in that old ass's pocket.

BERTRAND. Bitten, I think. (MACAIRE dancing mad.)

SCENE II

To these, DUMONT

DUMONT. Ah, friends, up so early? Catching the worm, catching the worm?

(Sitting on the table dissembling box and dissembling box . . .

MACAIRE. Good-morning, good-morning!

BERTRAND. Early birds, early birds.

DUMONT. By the way, very remarkable thing: I found the key.

MACAIRE. No!

BERTRAND. O!

DUMONT. Perhaps a still more remarkable thing: it was my key that had the twisted handle.

MACAIRE. I told you so.

DUMONT. Now, what we have to do is to get the cash-box. Hallo! what's that your sitting on?

BERTRAND. Nothing.

MACAIRE. The table! I beg your pardon.

DUMONT. Why, it's my cash-box!

MACAIRE. Why, so it is!

DUMONT. It's very singular.

MACAIRE. Diabolishly singular.

BERTRAND. Early worms, early worms!

DUMONT (blowing in key). Well, I suppose you are still willing to begone?

MACAIRE. More than willing, my dear soul: pressed, I may say, for time; for though it had quite escaped my memory, I have an appointment in Turin with a lady of title.

DUMONT (at box). It's very odd. (Blows its key.) It's a singular thing (blowing), key won't turn. It's a patent. Some one must have tampered with the lock (blowing). It's strangely singular, it's singularly singular! I've shown this key to commercial gentlemen all the way from Paris: they never saw a better key! (more business). Well (giving it up and looking reproachfully on key), that's pretty singular.

MACAIRE. Let me try. (He tries, and flings down the key with a curse.) Bitten.

BERTRAND. Sold again.

DUMONT (picking up key). It's a patent key.

MACAIRE (to BERTRAND). The game's up: we must save the swag. (To DUMONT.) Sir, since your key, on which I invoke the blight of Egypt, has once more defaulted, my feelings are unequal to a repetition of yesterday's distress, and I shall simply pad the hoof. From Turin you shall receive the address of my banker, and may prosperity attend your ventures. (To BERTRAND.) Now, boy! (To DUMONT.) Embrace my fatherless child! farewell! (MACAIRE and BERTRAND turn to go off and are met in the door by the GENDARMES.)

SCENE III

To these, the BRIGADIER and GENDARMES

BRIGADIER. Let no man leave the house.

MACAIRE (aside). Bitten.

BERTRAND (aside). Sold again.

DUMONT. Welcome, old friend!

BRIGADIER. It is not the friend that comes; it is the Brigadier. Summon your guests: I must investigate their passports. I am in pursuit of a notorious malefactor, Robert Macaire.

DUMONT. But I was led to believe that both Macaire and his accomplice had been arrested and condemned.

BRIGADIER. They were, but they have once more escaped for the moment, and justice is indefatigable. (He sits at table R.) Dumont, a bottle of white wine.

MACAIRE (to DUMONT). My excellent friend, I will discharge your commission, and return with all speed. (Going.)

BRIGADIER. Halt!

MACAIRE (returning: as if he saw BRIGADIER for the first time). Ha? a member of the force? Charmed, I'm sure. But you misconceive me: I return at once, and my friend remains behind to answer for me.

BRIGADIER. Justice is insensible to friendship. I shall deal with you in due time. Dumont, that bottle.

MACAIRE. Sir, my friend and I, who are students of character, would grasp the opportunity to share and may one add? to pay the bottle. Dumont, three!

BERTRAND. For God's sake! (Enter ALINE and MAIDS.)

MACAIRE. My friend is an author: so, in a humbler way, am I. Your knowledge of the criminal classes naturally tempts one to pursue so interesting an acquaintance.

BRIGADIER. Justice is impartial. Gentlemen, your health.

MACAIRE. Will not these brave fellows join us?

BRIGADIER. They are on duty; but what matters?

MACAIRE. My dear sir, what is duty? duty is my eye.

BRIGADIER (solemnly). And Betty Martin. (GENDARMES sit at table.)

MACAIRE (to BERTRAND). Dear friend, sit down.

BERTRAND (sitting down). O Lord!

BRIGADIER (to MACAIRE). You seem to be a gentleman of considerable intelligence.

MACAIRE. I fear, sir, you flatter. One has lived, one has loved, and one remembers: that is all. One's Lives of Celebrated Criminals has met with a certain success, and one is ever in quest of fresh material.

DUMONT. By the way, a singular thing about my patent key.

BRIGADIER. This gentleman is speaking.

MACAIRE. Excellent Dumont! he means no harm. This Macaire is not personally known to you?

BRIGADIER. Are you connected with justice?

MACAIRE. Ah, sir, justice is a point above a poor author.

BRIGADIER (with glass). Justice is the very devil.

MACAIRE. My dear sir, my friend and I, I regret to say, have an appointment in Lyons, or I could spend my life in this society. Charge your glasses: one hour to madness and to joy! What is to-morrow? the enemy of to-day. Wine? the bath of life. One moment: I find I have forgotten my watch. (He makes for the door.)

BRIGADIER. Halt!

MACAIRE. Sir, what is this jest?

BRIGADIER. Sentry at the door. Your passports.

MACAIRE. My good man, with all the pleasure in life. (Gives papers. The BRIGADIER puts on spectacles, and examines them.)

BERTRAND (rising, and passing round to MACAIRE'S other side). It's life and death: they must soon find it.

MACAIRE (aside). Don't I know? My heart's like fire in my body.

BRIGADIER. Your name is?

MACAIRE. It is; one's name is not unknown.

BRIGADIER. Justice exacts your name.

MACAIRE. Henri-Frédéric de Latour de Main de la Tonnerre de Brest.

BRIGADIER. Your profession?

MACAIRE. Gentleman.

BRIGADIER. No, but what is your trade?

MACAIRE. I am an analytical chymist.

BRIGADIER. Justice is inscrutable. Your papers are in order. (To BERTRAND.) Now, sir, and yours?

BERTRAND. I feel kind of ill.

MACAIRE. Bertrand, this gentleman addresses you. He is not one of us; in other scenes, in the gay and giddy world of fashion, one is his superior. But to-day he represents the majesty of law; and as a citizen it is one's pride to do him honour.

BRIGADIER. Those are my sentiments.

BERTRAND. I beg your pardon, I—(Gives papers.)

BRIGADIER. Your name?

BERTRAND. Napoleon.

BRIGADIER. What? In your passport it is written Bertrand.

BERTRAND. It's this way: I was born Bertrand, and then I took the name of Napoleon, and I mostly always call myself either Napoleon or Bertrand.

BRIGADIER. The truth is always best. Your profession?

BERTRAND. I am an orphan.

BRIGADIER. What the devil! (To MACAIRE.) Is your friend an idiot?

MACAIRE. Pardon me, he is a poet.

BRIGADIER. Poetry is a great hindrance to the ends of justice. Well, take your papers.

MACAIRE. Then we may go?

SCENE IV

To these, CHARLES, who is seen on the gallery, going to the door of Number Thirteen. Afterwards all the characters but the NOTARY and the MARQUIS

BRIGADIER. One glass more. (BERTRAND touches MACAIRE, and points to CHARLES, who enters Number Thirteen).

MACAIRE. No more, no more, no more.

BRIGADIER (rising and taking MACAIRE by the arm). I stipulate!

MACAIRE. Engagement in Turin!

BRIGADIER. Turin?

MACAIRE. Lyons, Lyons!

BERTRAND. For God's sake.

BRIGADIER. Well, good-bye!

MACAIRE. Good-bye, good—

CHARLES (from within). Murder! Help! (Appearing.) Help here! The Marquis is murdered.

BRIGADIER. Stand to the door. A man up there. (A GENDARME hurries up staircase into Number Thirteen, CHARLES following him. Enter on both sides of gallery the remaining characters of the piece, except the NOTARY and the MARQUIS.)

MACAIRE (aside). Bitten, by God!

BERTRAND (aside). Lost!

BRIGADIER (to DUMONT). John Paul Dumont, I arrest you.

DUMONT. Do your duty, officer. I can answer for myself and my own people.

BRIGADIER. Yes, but these strangers?

DUMONT. They are strangers to me.

MACAIRE. I am an honest man: I stand upon my rights: search me; or search this person, of whom I know too little. (Smiting his brow.) By heaven, I see it all! This morning—(To BERTRAND.) How, sir, did you dare to flaunt your booty in my very face? (To BRIGADIER.) He showed me notes; he was up ere day; search him, and you'll find. There stands the murderer.

BERTRAND. O, Macaire! (He is seized and searched and the notes are found.)

BRIGADIER. There is blood upon the notes. Handcuffs. (MACAIRE edging towards the door.)

BERTRAND. Macaire, you may as well take the bundle. (MACAIRE is stopped by sentry, and comes front, R.)

CHARLES (re-appearing). Stop, I know the truth. (He comes down.) Brigadier, my father is not dead. He is not even dangerously hurt. He has spoken. There is the would-be assassin.

MACAIRE. Hell! (He darts across to the staircase, and turns on the second step, flashing out the knife.) Back, hounds! (He springs up the stair, and confronts them from the top.) Fools, I am Robert Macaire! (As MACAIRE turns to flee, he is met by the gendarme coming out of Number Thirteen; he stands an instant checked, is shot from the stage, and falls headlong backward down the stair. BERTRAND, with a cry, breaks from the gendarmes, kneels at his side, and raises his head.)

BERTRAND. Macaire, Macaire, forgive me. I didn't blab; you know I didn't blab.

MACAIRE. Sold again, old boy. Sold for the last time; at least, the last time this side death. Death—what is death? (He dies.)

CURTAIN

www.ingramcontent.com/pod-product-compliance
Lightning Source LLC
Chambersburg PA
CBHW061439040426
42450CB00007B/1124